CREATIVE

Althea Pearson is a Cl.

private practice. Her first degree and doctorate, both in psychology,
were awarded by the University of London. She then gained a Diploma
in Counselling at the then Brighton Polytechnic.

She offers therapy to individuals and groups, as well as supervising
the work of other practitioners. In addition, she provides training and
personal growth activities in various settings, both locally and nationally,
and contributes to conferences and retreats.

Althea Pearson is married to Brian, who manages her psychology practice.
They have two sons. Her first book, Growing Through Loss
and Grief, was published in April 1994.

Other publications by Althea Pearson

Althea Pearson has written articles for the academic and popular press as
well as for the Christian press on aspects of psychology, mental health,
counselling and personal growth.

She was commissioned by HarperCollins Publishers to contribute two
titles to their series "Handbooks of Pastoral Care":
"Growing Through Loss and Grief" (1994) and "Creative Methods in
Counselling" (1997) (now reprinted in this edition).

She was a member of The Church of England House of Bishops'
Review Group on the Ministry of Healing, that produced:
"A Time to Heal. A Contribution towards the Ministry of Healing",
Church House Publishing (2000).

CREATIVE METHODS
IN COUNSELLING

Facilitating the healing process

ALTHEA PEARSON

Wild Duck Productions

Published by Wild Duck Productions

This edition 2007

3 5 7 9 10 8 6 4 2

Text Copyright © 1997 Althea Pearson

Woodspring Psychological Services
Tel: 0871 218 1977
Website: www.woodspringpsychology.co.uk

Cover Photograph and Design
Copyright © 2007 Wild Duck Productions

Wild Duck Productions
Tel: 0871 218 2183
Website: www.wildduckproductions.com

Althea Pearson asserts the moral right to be
identified as the author of this work

A catalogue record for this book is
available from the British Library

ISBN: 978-0-9556491-0-3

Printed by 4edge Ltd. Hockley. www.4edge.co.uk

CONTENTS

ACKNOWLEDGEMENTS
(written for 1st edition)

Many people are involved in the writing of a book of this kind and I am extremely grateful to them all.

My husband Brian is tremendously supportive of all my professional endeavours. My love and gratitude are boundless.

Thomas and Nicholas, our sons, are intrigued by my work and collect dolls and bric-a-brac from jumble sales saying 'It's for your room, Mum.' Wittingly and unwittingly they have also provided creative material for the book! For them, too, I have endless love and appreciation.

My mother has been an invaluable source of encouragement in all areas of my life, not least in producing this book. My love and grateful thanks go to her, as well as to other family members and friends who have expressed an interest in its progress.

Val Tilley, who typed much of this book, should be the one writing on the subject of creativity! Her notes to me are full of quirky wit and she has managed, against all the odds, to decipher and follow my instructions, such as my frequent decisions to alter the ordering of paragraphs. My heartfelt thanks go to her, for her unstinting hard work and unfailing good humour.

Kim Meacock produced the remainder of the typescript and for her calm smiles in the face of my requests to insert, remove or change sections, I am most grateful. She, too, apparently has a 'gift of interpretation' in that she has found her way through my scribbles, despite having no map!

Brenda Rogers, with whom I undertake peer supervision, has been a source of inspiration, helping me to cut through the inessentials to the nub of the truths I wish to convey. I am grateful to her for stimulating my cognitive and creative processes.

Christine Smith, until recently Editorial Director of Marshall Pickering, and Marlene Cohen, Series Editor, have made helpful comments about aspects of the manuscript. I have valued their support and clear thinking. Vicky Marquina, who edited the manuscript, has been meticulous about taking my wishes, for example regarding layout, into account.

I would like to extend enormous thanks to those clients, supervisees and others who have been willing to have their inner thoughts, feelings, dreams and aspirations exposed to your gaze. The truism holds good: without them there really would have been no book. Facilitating counselling, therapy and supervision is a huge privilege and I am tremendously grateful to have been allowed, not only to share their journeys, but also to extend that privilege to you. It has also been very humbling to find that every person I approached for permission to include material here agreed, and did so with selfless comments about '...if it can help other people...'.

Finally, I thank God for calling me to this work. May He bless all those mentioned here and may you, and those you counsel, also receive blessing.

ACKNOWLEDGEMENTS
(added for this edition)

Re-reading my original words, I find that everything that I wrote then still applies. In addition, I would like to mention others who have inspired me and contributed in a host of ways to the development of my thinking and therapeutic methods. It was Dr Chris Andrew and his wife, Pauline, who first introduced me to ways of working at depth and I am indebted to them and to others who have been involved, over the years, with Deep Release, the charity they set up.

For some years, my supervisor has been Marie Calvert and I have benefited hugely from her wisdom, gentleness and humour, coupled with honesty and enormous integrity. Her artistic gifts and originality are inspiring and enriching, and her eagerness to experiment with different ways of working is a great encouragement.

Our sons, now several years older, continue to delight and amaze me with their creativity in a number of areas. In particular, I should like to record my unstinting gratitude to them – and to my daughter-in-law, Davina – for their unfailingly helpful and patient responses when I have found myself stumped by some aspect of modern technology. And it is Tom and Davina – who as Wild Duck Productions – designed the cover for this new edition and who have generously granted me permission to use their photography for it.

Part One

SEEING THE WOOD FOR
THE TREES

Creativity and the Right Side of the Brain

'Write a sample chapter and outline of chapter contents.' It sounded straightforward when Christine Smith, the Editorial Director at Marshall Pickering, HarperCollins*Religious*, said it to me. I had met with her and Marlene Cohen, Series Editor, to discuss my second book in the series of Handbooks of Pastoral Care. I was pleased to have enthused them with my own keenness to write on creative methods of counselling. Producing a summary of contents and a draft chapter is the usual next step and the request came as no surprise. However, things did not go smoothly and in order to find a way forward I had to make use of an example of the very approach the book describes.

I quickly produced a first draft of the contents summary, then turned my attention to writing a sample chapter. When I write I do not start at page one and keep going until I complete the final page: I hop about, perhaps writing chapter six before chapter two and following up with chapter five. For the draft chapter, I decided to write one of the middle chapters, on Gestalt therapy, as this is an approach I draw on particularly often.

However…although I did manage to finish a chapter the result was leaden and Christine sent it back with gentle remarks about my style being different from the one I had used in my first book, *Growing Through Loss and Grief*. I didn't need to be told: I had *felt* the plodding nature of some of the writing. What's more, I knew what was wrong.

What was wrong had to do with the very nature of the subject matter. What I *didn't* know, though, was what to do about it.

One Brain, or Two?

The human brain is divided into two halves, or hemispheres, connected by a structure called the corpus callosum which relays messages between the two halves, thus allowing us to function as one person instead of two! (There exist heart-rending accounts in the medical and research literature of people who have had the corpus callosum cut through. For these people it is unfortunately true to say that 'the right hand doesn't know what the left hand is doing'. For example, they may simultaneously be putting on a sock with one hand and removing it with the other.) In a right-handed person, the left hemisphere is responsible for verbal functioning, and logical and linear thought processes. The right hemisphere, by contrast, is responsible for intuition, creativity and spatial processes. (For left-handers and mixed-handers the evidence, though not completely clear, suggests that the specialization of functions is less pronounced.)

This book considers creative processes; that is, it explores intuitive, non-linear processes – activities governed by the *right* side of the brain. Yet my committing them to paper requires verbal expression – a process carried out by the *left* side of my brain. Effectively, then, I was trying to force right side of brain activity into left side of brain expression – and the result was far from inspiring.

It was as though I was trying to translate material from one actual language into another. Much as I tried, this translation process was very difficult. I had to re-cast imagery, with multiple layers of symbolism, into words which (though they too are symbolic representations of things) nevertheless possess a harder, firmer, uni-dimensional identity. Other analogies are those of trying to find words to describe the quality of light before a storm, or one's emotional response to a piece of stirring music or to a profound experience of God. We grope for the right words but are frustrated by their inadequacy.

Do you remember that old advertisement for Cadbury's chocolate in which two jugsful of milk fitted happily into one smaller container? In the real world of accommodating ideas in words, only one jugful could possibly fit and for two months I had struggled to force the remaining jugful in – only to find milk pouring out in all directions!

Those words: 'Why don't you just think how you want the book to turn out, Mum?' had the catalytic effect of changing the shape and size of the container, so that it now held all the milk without half of it spilling out.

Alternatively, one could express this idea in terms taken from Gestalt. Gestalt is a German word with no exact English equivalent, but its meaning is roughly 'whole'. In Gestalt therapy one aims to close (or complete) Gestalts. A closed Gestalt takes on an enriched life of its own and a further Gestalt concept often becomes clear, which is that 'the whole is greater than the sum of the parts'. So it could be said that the effect of Thomas' words was to close one incomplete Gestalt which had been pushing for closure for two months, while opening up another more creatively useful Gestalt. The new Gestalt (or container!) allows me to present the material I wish to cover in ways which will be more creative, and therefore truer to the subject matter.

The book's form of presentation – which will still, by necessity and definition, be the written word – will remain linear. But its *order* of presentation will not be exclusively linear. Sometimes I will allow two jugs (or more, if necessary) to flow into one container, presenting the resulting Gestalt, rather than attempting to discuss – *in isolation* – the contribution of just one of those jugs. Or, to return to an earlier analogy, the bag is now closed over the puppy who, though still boisterous, is no longer uncontrollable.

2 Not Seeing the Wood for the Trees

Thomas' question provided the means I needed to identify the relevant Gestalt. I had been concentrating on the component parts, but these had not fitted into a coherent whole because 'the whole is greater than the sum of the parts'. That is, two separate jugsful of milk actually produce *more* than two jugsful, not *less*.

Another way of expressing part of this can be captured in the saying 'I can't see the wood for the trees'. It was as though I was too busy concentrating on individual trees to remember to look at the overall wood. Often, my clients are in a similar predicament: they know that something is out of kilter or needs re-aligning – but are unable to identify what needs to change, or how to effect that change.

Then, my job is to help them discover the 'what?' – after which the 'how?' usually falls relatively easily into place. And – in best 'physician heal thyself' tradition – one of the ways I may help clients is by making just the sort of intervention that Thomas made. His questions helped me to grasp again the shape of the wood, which allowed me to see the trees more clearly.

What are 'Creative Methods'?

Thomas' words to me, 'How do you want your book to turn out, Mum?' functioned as a creative question, in much the same way that creative methods of counselling can move clients on – in their thinking, attitudes, imagination, emotions or the degree to which a problem has been resolved. That question helped me identify the missing link, and was the catalyst which helped me put my wordless struggle into words. Making intangible things concrete is often a hallmark of creative methods of counselling. In that respect, creative methods can be anything that has these effects.

Of course, active listening, Rogerian counselling, mirroring and other approaches which could be subsumed under the heading 'the talking cure' can be used creatively and can be powerful tools in a counsellor's hands. But there is a plethora of books on counselling in a more or less Rogerian mode, whereas there are far fewer books on creative methods, and none that I know of which has been written specifically for Christians. I am using the term 'creative methods' to indicate those techniques and approaches which take account of right side of brain activities and functioning. Use of symbolism, the imagination and intuition can all play a part, being welcomed and fostered, rather than ignored. So Thomas' question encouraged me to use my imagination to picture the actual completed book and to find a dynamic symbolic representation of it. Having done that I was finally able to find a way through my predicament. I also knew how to reach the goal which I could see clearly at last.

By relying solely on left side of brain functions we render unconscious material less accessible and so run the risk of encouraging clients to utilize defence methods such as intellectualization and rationalization. This can even mean that we inadvertently reinforce the very tendencies which caused people to ask for help in the first place. That is, a person who tends to over-intellectualize and to try to find logical explanations when they cannot always be found, may not be best helped by a form of counselling based on those processes. Instead, counselling of this kind may prove intensely frustrating for both the people involved, with neither quite knowing why.

If, instead, we invite people to use and value the functions of the right side of their brains, we can facilitate change at a deeper level, as they integrate parts of themselves which had previously been split off from each other. Such splits may reveal themselves in phrases like, 'I *know* God loves me but I don't feel it.' When a person is saying something like this, working with them at a purely cognitive level is likely to bring nothing but frustration – and a sense of banging our heads against a brick wall – for them and us. By contrast, the use of methods which make room for both the cognitive *and* the affective (emotional); both the rational *and* the intuitive; in short, both the left *and* right sides of the brain, is likely to be far more fruitful.

Sometimes these 'creative methods' can involve verbal material, for example in the form of metaphor and simile. Symbols, whether of this kind or visual, can express profound, complex notions incredibly succinctly. My current favourite, whose unexpected occurrence made it even more amusing, stands for a church (perhaps even for the Church). One friend has what is politely known as an 'ample bosom' and, in an attempt to reduce the apparent size of her bust, has taken to wearing a 'minimizing bra'. She suddenly said to me one day, 'The Church does the same as my bra does.' 'What, squash you flat?' I asked. 'No,' she replied, 'instead of uplifting and supporting me, it takes what God has given me and squeezes it into a different mould.'

Symbolism in Scripture

The Gospels make it clear that Jesus frequently engaged with the imaginative, intuitive parts of a person by the frequency with which they record His use of imagery. It is in the parables that we find Jesus making greater use of verbal symbolism, but there are other instances such as His words: 'It is easier for a camel to go through the eye of a needle than for a rich man to enter the Kingdom of God' (Matthew 19:24).

Personally, I find another form of Jesus' use of symbols even more telling. These occur when Jesus Himself *is* the symbol, such as when He washes the disciples' feet (John 13:1–11).

Our liturgy and Church traditions, too, carry great symbolism; from the 'All we like sheep have gone astray' of the *Book of Common Prayer*, to 'He opened wide His arms for us on the cross' of the ASB: and from the use of candles to the pastoral staff carried by a bishop.

Why Use Creative Methods?

The field of counselling is mushrooming; innovative approaches are being introduced all the time. I think it was Larry Norman, the Christian songwriter, who said 'Why should the devil have all the best music?' and I want to extend that sentiment to the field of counselling.

There have been many attempts to classify different temperament types. One which has received a lot of attention, particularly in Church circles, is the Myers-Briggs Type Indicator®.[1] Its roots are in Jungian analysis, and also in a much earlier understanding of people. Briefly, people are regarded as preferring one or other pole of four sets of polarities. One of these – iNtuition vs Thinking – has considerable bearing on the current discussion. Apparently, the proportion of N's in the churches is far higher than outside; and N's make sense of the world largely through iNtuitive processes. Therefore, to facilitate fully and appropriately a person who has a preference towards the iNtuitive function, we need to bring our own iNtuitive processes to bear. I speak as an N – which is another reason why I am writing a book on this topic!

Profound elements of our Judaeo-Christian tradition have been hijacked by other groups over the years. The sign of the rainbow, a reminder from God to his people that He keeps His promises, has been adopted as a New Age logo, while that most sacred of Christian symbols, the cross, turns up in all sorts of settings. Other groups may have chosen to use the Judaeo-Christian symbols for their own purposes, but it seems to me that we are in danger of jettisoning the profound worth of those same symbols, and the context in which they, and all the other symbolism and imagery, were given.

I am referring to the hesitation which some Christians feel over making use of techniques which utilize the imagination, or even symbolism. From that strangely moving image of the Spirit brooding over the deep, in the opening paragraphs of Genesis, to Revelation with its extraordinary picture language, the Bible contains an astonishing wealth of symbolism. By its very nature, symbolism can be fully appreciated only by use of the imagination. Concepts such as camels going through the eyes of needles, God judging a city by using a plumb line, arrays of golden lampstands: none of these can be comprehended by the logical, left side of our brain, but only by the imaginative, right side of our brain. This is how we have been created, and this is how God has expressed Himself in His Word.

There are many creative, potentially useful ways to help people to find a way through their problems. Christians owe it to themselves, to the people they are seeking to help, and to God to learn about these techniques. It is my conviction that our creativity and imagination are God-given. Therefore, I believe that God intends us to use them to benefit ourselves and others. While Christians are undoubtedly wise to steer clear of techniques which stem from magic, New Age beliefs or mind control, some try to extend this to an (impossible to achieve) avoidance of more or less anything which has its roots in secular insights. Sadly, one has only to acknowledge the flights of imagination pursued in real life by torturers to acknowledge that God's gift to human beings of imagination – in common with His other gifts – is open to abuse. But to my mind it would be throwing out the baby with the bath water to eschew creative approaches to counselling on the grounds that some come from the imagination.

Naturally, we will want to monitor techniques, which may lead to our adapting or avoiding some. Overall, though, they can expand and enhance our counselling practice – and undoubtedly can be used as a powerful vehicle by God, the ultimate creator.

The Layout of the Book

In essence, this is a practical 'how to' book in which I will introduce a number of techniques and suggest and demonstrate various ways of using them. It would have been possible to write a practical book which was just that – all techniques and no theoretical justification or scriptural perspective. However, to my mind, such a book would have limited usefulness, so Part One provides the theoretical content and biblical underpinnings of these approaches.

Creative techniques are next considered individually in Part Two in order to show some of the range of possible uses of each. Part Three then demonstrates how different techniques can be used at different times with the same person. This approach is hopefully true to the message contained in the image of the tall figure in the rich, swirling cloak. A seamless, moving cloak, though exciting and vibrant, may have proved difficult for you, the reader, to handle. Instead, I aim to provide close inspection of sections of the cloak as seen through a magnifying glass – but at other times (especially in the final Part) I will show the whole cloak.

A Suggestion

If you are a person who opens a book and flicks through until something catches your eye, then you may never read this suggestion!

If you are someone who opens the front cover of a book and reads methodically through then this suggestion does not apply to you!

If you are a person who reads the opening chapter of a book and then flicks back and forth through the rest, I suggest you make a point of reading at least Part One first. Acquaint yourself with the material contained in these chapters before starting to 'flick', as they provide the contextual framework which will render the rest of the book both more useful and more comprehensible.

1. Isabel Briggs Myers, *Introduction to Type*, Consulting Psychologists Press Inc., Palo Alto, CA 94303, USA, 1987.

2

SHEEP AND SHEAVES; LAMBS
AND LAMPSTANDS

*Symbols, Metaphors and Picture Language
in the Bible*

When I was at school, finding French lessons to be something of a
struggle, I used to hope I would marry someone who was bilingual so
our children could learn two languages from the cradle and avoid a
nightmare similar to the one I was going through. (I didn't and so they
didn't. Besides, in time, other qualities in a potential husband took on
far greater significance!) In a similar way, I sometimes think that growing up as an Orthodox Jew and then becoming a Christian would have
huge advantages in providing a thorough grounding in the Old
Testament, and in Judaic beliefs. (Both fantasies, of course, ignore the
possible drawbacks such as trying to straddle two cultures, or facing
rejection by one's family.)

From Sunday School days I have been taught that the 'Bible is full
of picture language' and I am painfully aware of how little of it I
understand. It is a source of great pleasure to me to have the scriptures opened up, rather as Jesus did for the two disciples on the
Emmaus road (Luke 24:27). Invariably, puzzling bits have light
thrown upon them, or – perhaps even more satisfying – the import of
passages about which I had been in ignorance is revealed. Those
moments have something about them which reminds me of the rend-
ing of the curtain in the Holy of Holies (Luke 23:45), or the 'something like scales' falling from Saul's eyes (Acts 9:18). They are

moments when I suddenly perceive truths of which I had previously been unaware – such as the symbolic significance of the crucifixion. It took place at the time of the Passover feast, when the Jews were bringing their perfect lambs to Jerusalem. Then Jesus – the Passover Lamb – was sacrificed (1 Corinthians 5:7).

Some of the gems which can be mined in the scriptures are to be dug out with the tools of *insight* into cultural practices and customs. Many sermons preached by my husband have stayed with me over the years, but perhaps none more so than one on the twenty-third psalm. Hearing him expound the cultural significance of such phrases as the 'Valley of the Shadow of Death' (a real route through a mountain range. At one point the path is divided by a gully. Sheep have to jump across, coaxed by the shepherd); and anointing 'my head with oil' (as each sheep enters the sheepfold it is examined for thorns and scratches. The shepherd puts olive oil on any injury) was a very moving experience. Its factual content appealed to the left side of my brain, while I responded intuitively from the right side of my brain to its personal implications.

At other times, the riches in a passage of the Bible are revealed when a writer or speaker mines the seam of a symbol with a well established *interpretation* which would have been known to people of the day. Certain numbers, for example, were regarded in particular ways, with seven being the number of completeness. A Jew, then, would take particular note of occurrences of the number seven in scripture. (It appears 52 times in the Book of Revelation alone.) By contrast, it would be very easy indeed for a twentieth-century Westerner to be blind to much scriptural symbolism through ignorance of this fact.

Biblical Garden

When he had the opportunity to stay for a week at a study centre in Israel, my husband was greatly enriched by the experiences he had, and by the teaching he received. He wrote:

The first lesson I learnt during my 'study pilgrimage' was the existence of the 'fifth Gospel'. This, I was told, is the country itself, the backcloth to the Gospel accounts which we know as Israel or the Holy Land. But it is not just the physical terrain; it is the history, the culture, the language, the customs and the very way of living of the people who inhabited that compact but diverse territory.

With great care and precision, a team of American biblical archaeologists had created a garden in part of the grounds of an ecumenical study centre a few kilometres outside Jerusalem on the way to Bethlehem. My first tour of the garden was a guided one and enabled me to become familiar with the setting, structures, uses and biblical contexts of the 'exhibits'. But for the remainder of my stay this garden became a place of reflection and contemplation, a place of discovery and illumination, as familiar biblical references moved from the written page and memory to visible, tangible representations within sight and reach.

The well with large stone water pots alongside, the threshing floor with implements studded with metal and flint – the same used to scourge our Lord – and the vine press, with its channels stained claret, all these 'spoke' scripture to me, presented deeper meaning and offered new insights. The watchtower, the sheep-gate and the cisterns moved from being mere visual aids to dramatic prompts which located familiar stories in a present experience as well as an ancient narrative.

Of course, an illustrated Bible had presented these 'pictures' to me from childhood. Later, 3-D models and replicas provided further clarity but there, in the land, is the fifth Gospel itself, where I not only saw a manger (stone, of course, not wood) but touched it and smelt it. As I entered the tiny stable outside which it stood, meaning and understanding were transformed into a spiritual rather than cerebral experience.

Each day I spent some time in the garden. I moved to a different place – under the fig tree, on the different soils for the Sower Parable, beside the oil-press – and lived the scripture not only in my mind and imagination but in my heart and my soul. Even when, after a week or so, my itinerary took me on to the glorious and powerful setting of Lake Galilee, my thoughts travelled back often – as they still do – to the Biblical Garden and the spiritual encounters that became such an integral and formative part of my journey of faith.

One Biblical Theme: Water

Learning about the significance and importance of various people, places and practices in Jewish history, tradition and thought can add multiple layers to scriptural passages which we had found baffling or which had seemed one-dimensional.

Take the theme of water, for example. Even the most cursory glance at the Jewish context reveals the fact that water was an extremely precious commodity. The theme of abundant spiritual blessings symbolized by quantities of water occurs repeatedly in John's Gospel: for example, the streams of living water, 7:38; and the woman at the well, 4:14. Water recurs as a main feature in the account of Jesus walking on the water (6:19). This passage contains deeper symbolism, showing Jesus' supernatural supremacy over the natural elements. Most notable, though, is the account of the wedding at Cana (2:1–11), which is a multi-layered image of plenitude, as the amount of wine (and water) was huge, and was provided when guests had already drunk a good deal.

Time and again throughout the scriptures, the cultural necessity of strict conservation of a scarce resource is overturned in the use of water as a symbol of God's abundance. Jesus' words about streams of living water welling up in Christians are prefigured, for example, in Psalm 107:35: 'He turned the desert into pools of water'.

Then there are rivers: in the Garden of Eden (Genesis 2:10); flowing from the new temple (Ezekiel 47); and in the New Jerusalem (Revelation 22:1, 2).

I find I get most satisfyingly 'fed' by the Bible when I appreciate more than one of the layers at which a particular passage functions. For example, in Isaiah 43:2 God promises to be with His people when they 'pass through the waters' and that the rivers 'will not sweep over' them. Taking that passage literally, 'waters' would be interpreted as wet stuff essential for survival yet deadly in excess. (Before dismissing this as an unlikely meaning in the context of the passage, we need to be aware of the huge importance of the crossing of the Red Sea in the history of Isaiah's first hearers. Their escape from slavery, possibly their very survival as a nation, and certainly their entry into the Promised Land had all depended on the waters not 'sweeping over them'. So the elements of survival and threat are clearly represented; indeed, Isaiah goes on – in the same chapter – to make a clear reference to the crossing of the Red Sea.)

If you read the passage at a different level, you can make connections between 'water' and being overwhelmed by something powerful, even elemental. In either case you may respond with thankful *thoughts* that God promises to uphold and protect you, but you will probably not yet have *felt* it. If, instead, you allow yourself to enter fully into the imagery of threat to your life; of struggling to survive a near-drowning, you will become more fully aware of the potential impact of the passage.

Let's stay with the drowning theme for a little longer. For me, the most meaningful sermons on the Storm on the Lake (Mark 4:35–41) have been those which have acknowledged Jesus' power, not only over the elements, but over our lesser 'storms'. To be reminded that Jesus cares about and wants to calm our fears and anxieties, and to bring the peace of His presence into 'stormy' relationships and situations is more directly relevant than to hear the incident treated as 'only' a miracle over nature.

Biblical truths speak to our spirits and build us up, and can be used therapeutically in various ways. At the end of this chapter I include a transcript of an audio tape made for a friend on the theme of water. Suddenly bereaved, he was experiencing sleeping difficulties and I offered to make a tape which would induce sleep. When embarking on any relaxation exercise, I ask the person concerned about scenes or activities they find relaxing. My friend said 'a warm bath' – which instantly provided the theme of water.

Other Symbols in the Bible

There are many other motifs in scripture, such as light, brides, lambs or stones, the study of which reveal deeply meaningful truths. In addition to the themes which thread their way right through the scriptures there are many passages – even whole books – which contain powerful symbolism. The Song of Songs and the Book of Revelation, of course, contain large amounts of that 'picture language' referred to earlier. Then there are the passages based around actual experiences:

for example, Jeremiah's visit to the potter's house (Jeremiah 18, 19); the feeding of the 5,000 (Luke 9:10–17); the burning bush (Exodus 3:2); or Elijah and the prophets of Baal (1 Kings 18). Many of the great changes in the lives of individuals and communities were also ushered in as 'picture language': for example, Peter's vision of the great sheet (Acts 10:9–16); Joseph's dreams of wheat sheaves, sun, moon and stars (Genesis 37:5–9); and his interpretation of the Pharaoh's dreams (Genesis 41).

Perhaps the clearest metaphors are those in which God uses actual objects, events and people as the elements in symbolism. The story of Jeremiah's linen belt (Jeremiah 13:1–11), its purchase, burial and ruination, is immediately interpreted by God who says He will ruin the pride of the people of Judah and Jerusalem who would not be bound to Him.

Of all the examples of action analogy, probably the starkest in the Old Testament is the story of Hosea who was told to marry a prostitute, who continued to be unfaithful to him; while in the New Testament the image of Jesus crucified clearly carries the strongest impact.

Conclusion

Throughout the Bible, then, instances abound of the 'picture language' which we have heard referred to since we were children.

Some of these instances of biblical symbolism can be interpreted at various levels, while others (such as much of the Book of Revelation) are virtually impenetrable to the processes of the left side of the brain. Our own culture values logical, rational pursuits more highly than intuitive, creative ones. We are affected by this, and from schooldays onwards we learn to adapt our reactions so as to demonstrate more left side of brain activity and less from the right side of the brain. This can mean that we reduce the impact which biblical passages would otherwise have on us. That is, we learn to perceive only the straightforward meanings contained in scripture, by splitting off our creative and affective responses. In so doing we demean ourselves and dilute the message and power of the Bible. The Bible is the Word of God – the expression of Himself – and that Word contains more than words. We are not only thinking, speaking beings, but feeling, imagining, experiencing ones as well. And we have been created in God's image.

I cannot stress too strongly that scripture cannot be received and understood by logical analysis alone. Instead, God wants us to bring our *whole* selves to His Word and to Himself.

And, similarly, we cannot appreciate, understand or help ourselves or other people by using logical processes alone. Instead, I urge you to enter into the creative, sometimes playful, certainly revealing approaches governed by the right side of the brain, and to experience the unlocking of material (and releasing of lives) which they evoke.

A Sleep Tape, Based on the Theme of Water

This tape is designed to help you to relax into refreshing sleep, and should be read slowly.

First I suggest that you find a position which is comfortable for sleeping...it may be on your side, or your back or your front: whatever is most comfortable for you, adopt that position now.

Be aware that your mind and spirit can relax now, too. Your body, mind and spirit are being handed into God's safekeeping. Allow him to take all the concerns and cares which might otherwise preoccupy you. Be conscious now of offering those things to him as you sleep.

Now take some time to consciously and deliberately focus your attention on each part of your body in turn. Begin with your feet. Take your attention to your toes. Let them become soft and loose, not scrunched up or stretched out, just soft and relaxed.

Then let your ankles relax.

The feeling of relaxation is spreading into your calves now. They are soft and relaxed.

Now let your knees soften and loosen. Your lower legs are feeling very relaxed now.

That feeling of relaxation is spreading into your thighs – let them become soft and heavy.

And now let your buttocks soften. The weight of your whole

lower body is held by the bed – you don't have to do anything at all to support yourself.

Now this feeling of relaxation is spreading into your lower back. Let your back soften – it doesn't have to be arched or stiff – just let it relax.

And then let that feeling of relaxation flow into your stomach. Let those muscles soften and relax.

Now the relaxation is spreading to your upper back. Let the mattress take your whole weight. Enjoy the sense of your whole back being relaxed.

Your chest, too, is soft and relaxed.

You're becoming very relaxed now.

This feeling is spreading across your shoulders. If you are carrying any tension there, just gently tense them, then release. Your shoulders are very relaxed now.

The feeling of relaxation is spreading down your arms. They are soft and loose. Your hands, too, are relaxed. Your wrists and fingers are soft.

Now take your attention to your neck. Soften your neck and feel the relaxation spread up into your scalp.

The weight of your head is taken by your pillow. Relax into that now.

Your forehead is softening. Let your eyebrows relax at a comfortable mid-point, not held too high or pulled too low.

Be aware of the relaxation spreading to your eyes. Relax the little muscles around them so that you feel your eyes softening.

Your cheeks, too, are softening.

Relax your upper lip, and let your tongue soften – it need not be pressed against the roof of your mouth, nor against its floor. The whole area of your mouth is soft now.

Now your whole body is enjoying a wonderful sense of relaxation.

Take your attention back round your body to detect any knots of tension which may have crept back. And relax them…You're very relaxed now.

Imagine that you're going to enjoy a long soak in a warm bath. Imagine walking into the warm bathroom, putting in the plug and turning on the taps. You can hear the water splashing into the bath and you can see the steam start to rise.

Now you can decide what else to put into your bath: perhaps something to make bubbles, or to make the water feel silky, or something that just smells nice. Whatever is your choice, put it in now.

As you watch and listen to the water running into the bath, be aware of Jesus' words: 'Whoever believes in me, as the scripture has said, streams of living water will flow from within him.' By this he meant the Spirit, whom those who believed in Him were later to receive.

And as you stand now, watching and listening as the water flows into the bath, give thanks to God for the Spirit who is within you.

The water level is almost high enough now. Just test the temperature with your hand. Make sure it's comfortable for you: neither too hot nor too cold. Then, slowly, get into the water.

Just as you felt that sense of relaxation passing from one part of your body to the next, so now you feel the warmth of the water move from your feet, up your body, as you settle into this relaxing bath.

As you sink into the water, be aware of just relaxing into God; relaxing into the warmth of His love and of His acceptance. And as you think of this water, think, too, of His power over water:

...of Him dividing the waters of the Red Sea;

...and of Jesus walking on the water.

And offer to God any situation which needs His powerful, dividing touch, so you can walk through safely on dry ground. Or bring to Him any situation in your life over which you need to glide, but fear you may drown.

So enjoy this bath. Savour the fragrance and the warmth. Enjoy that sense of breathing in the steam and know, as you do this, that you are also breathing in the Spirit of God: His acceptance of you, His forgiveness: whatever you need, you can breathe it in from Him now.

Unlike most water, this water is safe for you to sleep in. Its temperature will remain constant and it will buoy you up, because 'underneath are the everlasting arms'. So you can relax into sleep in this water, in safety and comfort. And, as you do, think of these words:

But now, this is what the Lord says – He who created you, O Jacob,
He who formed you, O Israel:
'Fear not, for I have redeemed you;
I have summoned you by name; you are mine.
When you pass through the waters,
I will be with you;
and when you pass through the rivers,
they will not sweep over you.
For I am the Lord, your God,
the Holy one of Israel, your Saviour;
you are precious and honoured in my sight,
and I love you.
Do not be afraid, for I am with you.'

So, now take this sense of complete peace and relaxation of body, mind and spirit and allow yourself to move into a state of sleep. Drift off to sleep now, still with this safe water around you. Bathed, just as though back in the womb, in these safe, protective waters. And know how precious you are in the sight of God. May God bless you.

Texts used: John 7:38, 39; Deuteronomy 33:27; selections from Isaiah 43:1–5.

3

PUT YOURSELF IN MY PLACE

Some Uses of Chair Work

We have all heard the dictum 'put yourself in the other person's shoes' and recognize the increased empathy which can come from doing so. Putting oneself in another person's place can be extremely helpful and enlightening, especially as an antidote to judgemental feelings.

Sometimes when I am teaching counselling I show a postcard I was once given, with the familiar words of a Native American Indian prayer: 'Great Spirit, grant that I may not criticize my neighbour until I have walked a mile in his moccasins.'

Counsellors from various backgrounds use this idea of putting oneself in another person's place to help people increase their perspective. They do so in various ways. Some use verbal methods in order to encourage this widening of viewpoint, such as asking a person how other people would be affected by an action of theirs, such as divorce or a change of job. Those with a Transactional Analysis or Gestalt training, as well as some others, not only take the phrase 'put yourself in their place' figuratively, but – as far as is possible – also take it literally. That is, they make use of changes of body position to facilitate insight and resolution. Specifically, they invite clients to move to a different chair when taking the role of another person. Physically moving in this way facilitates the process of separating the various strands. This unravelling allows the person to perceive with greater clarity the contribution of the different elements to the overall picture.

Chair Work and Gestalt

It requires considerable time, training and commitment to become a Gestalt therapist, but some of the principles and techniques of Gestalt therapy can be usefully employed by other counsellors and therapists. One such approach is that of two-chair work.[1]

Fritz Perls, the originator of Gestalt therapy, utilized this technique as a way of externalizing people's projections. A person places on a chair in front of them (in their imagination) a person, concept, dream character, project, illness or anything else with which (or whom) the person has an issue to address. Then, talking to it (or him or her), the strands of the problem become clearer, and resolution becomes possible.

Judy was a successful businesswoman yet had suddenly found herself prevaricating over finishing work on a particular project. She put that project 'in the chair' and addressed it: 'I need you,' she said. 'I need you as a backdrop to give me self-importance and status. Once you're finished the company may decide they don't need me any more. So you have to stay incomplete or my job may be on the line.' In Judy's case, insight came remarkably quickly. More usually, a certain amount of swapping between chairs and 'personae' is required. The counsellor's job is to help the person stay rooted in the 'here and now': to speak in the present tense and in the first person and to report and express feelings and reactions as they occur *now* (not to talk about feelings from the past). In so doing the counsellor follows closely all that the client says and does, remembering that when verbal and non-verbal messages are in conflict the non-verbal messages are more likely to be accurate.

Just as becoming a Gestalt therapist requires considerable commitment, so becoming a qualified Transactional Analyst also takes considerable time, training and dedication – yet the basic principles of TA are useful for any counsellor as background knowledge to be frequently called upon and as tools to be occasionally brought out.

Transactional Analysts work with the concepts of Parent, Adult and Child as representing parts ('ego-states') present in all of us.[2] From early childhood each person is deemed to have certain 'ego-states'. These are defined as 'a consistent pattern of feeling and experience

directly related to a corresponding consistent pattern of behaviour.'³
These ego-states are:

The Adult, who carries out processes concerned with testing out
reality: organizing, using logic and rationality to assess and to deal with
reality.

The Parent, which is 'a set of feelings, attitudes, and behaviour patterns which resemble those of a parental figure'.⁴ Functionally it is
divided into *Critical* (or *Controlling*) Parent, who admonishes, punish-
es, uses words such as 'ought', 'should', 'must', and elicits feelings of
anxiety and worthlessness in the Child; and *Nurturing* Parent, who
'comforts, soothes, praises, and provides the stability that allows the
Child to be spontaneous, creative, kind and considerate.' The function
of the Parent is to 'provide a set of values and standards for behaviour
for the individual and, therefore, to conserve energy and diminish anxiety'.⁵

The Child, which is 'a set of feelings, attitudes, and behaviour patterns which are relics of the individual's own childhood'.⁶ It is divided
into *Free* (or *Natural*) Child and *Adapted* Child. A. Lorean Roberts
describes these as follows: 'The Natural Child strives for total freedom, to do what it wants to do it when it wants to do it. It has natural
impulses for love, affection, creativity, aggression, and rebellion, and
it acts spontaneously. The Adapted Child, on the other hand, is influ-
enced by the parent and it has discovered ways, usually compliance,
avoidance or procrastination, to deal with feelings in a manner which
will not bring forth parental reprimand. The Adapted Child duplicates
the original reactions the individual had towards his parents during
childhood, and holds feelings such as guilt, fright, sullenness, confusion, and other childlike emotions.'⁷

There are numerous therapeutic situations in which resolving conflicts
between these parts, or bringing integration to them is required. One
possible technique is that of conducting a conversation between the
ego-states:

For example, Paul, a student, was experiencing difficulty in maintaining a responsible, Christian standard of sexual behaviour and felt he had let himself, his family and God down by sleeping with other students. When he moved between different chairs, voicing the thoughts and feelings peculiar to each, it became clear that his Child ego-state enjoyed the thrill of doing something 'naughty' while his Parent ego-state strongly disapproved. His Adult ego-state functioned as a referee while he worked at strengthening his resolve to find some other form of excitement than promiscuity.

A useful group activity is to invite group members to take a chair each; giving themselves sufficient room to move comfortably around it. They then move to different compass points, shifting into each ego-state at each new position, and from that place addressing themselves (in the chair) verbally, or subvocally.

One man could calmly hear messages from his Adult and Adapted Child and Nurturing Parent ('Lots of children get hit'; 'I'll try to be good' and 'Don't cry') but was moved to tears by the messages from his Free (Hurt) Child and Critical Parent ('Don't hit me!' and 'I'll beat you senseless, you little wretch!').

Having broken through this barrier he was then able to do much useful therapeutic work, confronting his abusive father (in the chair) and later, having his Inner Child nurtured by being comforted by another group member who took the part of a Nurturing Parent. ('Re-parenting' does not seek to dispel old memories and facts about a person's life and replace them with fantasies, but to enlarge their Parent ego-state and so increase their repertoire of behaviours, feelings and beliefs.)

In addition to these dialogues or conversations between different parts of the person, Transactional Analysts also use chairs to facilitate conversations between the therapist and some other person who, though not actually present, nevertheless exerts an important influence on the client.

For example, it is quite common for a Transactional Analyst to conduct a 'parent interview'.[8] Here, the client is asked to move to a different chair and to adopt the persona of one or other parent. The therapist then speaks to the client as if he or she were this other person, for example, their mother or grandfather. In so doing, the therapist and client discover the content of the client's Parent ego-state.

In the process of being interviewed in, as it were, the 'shoes' of this person, the client typically gains insight into the dynamics which have been operating. A man who seeks help with overworking may have assumed that his father approved of his hard work and would disapprove if he were to ease up a bit. He may then be quite surprised to realize, at a different level of understanding, that actually his father encouraged him to work hard at school, but now would be relieved to see his son relax a little. Suddenly, an outmoded belief structure is seen for what it is: *previously* useful, authentic and relevant – but now inappropriate.

Change of this kind simply does not seem to occur – or certainly does not happen so quickly – using only verbal counselling methods. There is something intrinsically releasing about body movement. When a person gets up and goes to sit in another chair, the scene is set for swifter, more profound shifts of understanding, insight and the resolve to change.

Putting Jesus 'In the Chair'

One variation of chair work which I have found to be particularly powerful is to suggest that a Christian puts him or herself in Jesus' place. Sadly, harsh upbringing or specific traumas can affect the view people have of God. Much of our perception of God stems from attitudes, emotions and beliefs which originate in those we hold about our parents (or other important authority figures). So, for example, most survivors of childhood abuse perpetrated by their fathers experience huge difficulty in believing in a 'loving heavenly father' and instead expect humiliation, unforgiveness for even petty misdemeanours and cruelty. The use only of verbal methods may serve simply to reinforce this negative view of God. Chair work, by contrast, in which the person talks to God (or Jesus) and then changes chairs and speaks *as* Him can encourage the person into less negative views. This method also allows more room for the Holy Spirit to break through, sometimes in the most unexpected, beautiful way.

Matthew was a retired businessman. He felt that his wh
been blighted by the fact that his father (now in his eighties)
loved him. We worked on this in various ways, including ‚
father in the chair, first to blame and then to forgive him. Matthew also
swapped chairs and experienced 'being' his father responding to the
things his son had said. Back in his own chair, Matthew became tearful
as resentment gave way to compassion.

I then brought another chair forward and suggested that he imagine
Jesus on it, looking at Matthew and his father. Matthew first spoke to
Jesus and then took Jesus' place and spoke both to himself (Matthew)
and to his father. Matthew reported experiencing profound healing
from this, receiving a deep sense of forgiveness and restoration for
himself and being very moved by being given what amounted to
prophetic words for both himself and his father.

A year or so ago I was introduced to a technique by Brigid Proctor
involving putting oneself in the other person's place. Participants in
the workshop were asked to get into pairs and each person facilitated
his or her partner.

The technique is simple yet powerful. It involves putting 'on the
chair' a person one is having difficulty with, or finding hard to understand. Wordlessly observe the person (that is, the empty chair) for a
few moments, then change places and be the person looking back at
yourself. Then step away from both chairs and look in on the two figures represented by the two chairs. Finally, step back further and
observe yourself as you observe the two people you are imagining in
the chairs. It so happened that, on the day of the workshop, the person
I was having most 'difficulty' with was Jesus! So I put Him on the chair.
When I then took His place, my resentments melted away, as I felt the
deep love He had for me.

Although not set up specifically as a technique for Christians, done
in this way the exercise reminds me of the story of a man in hospital
who was dying. He told a trusted visitor that he was not alone: Jesus
often came and sat on the chair next to him. Asked what passed
between them, the man simply replied: 'I looks at Him and He looks
at me.' When he died, he was found leaning out of bed, his arms
embracing the chair.

Chair Work and Decision Making

Chair work can also be used to facilitate decision making. When people feel 'stuck', not knowing how to proceed because of the conflicting messages in their heads, greater clarity can be achieved by having them place chairs in a row or circle. As they move to sit in the position of each message, they make a statement about the decision that 'fits' that position. The chairs usually represent ego-states but could equally well represent sub-personalities, family members, colleagues or whatever. The point here is to tease out the various strands in order to see them more clearly.

People then may realize that the real conflict exists between two of the 'chairs' (people, ideas): the rest are 'red herrings', which are confusing the real issue. Or, when using chairs as ego-states, people realize they have been paying an inappropriate amount of attention to the messages from one of their ego-states and decide to redress that balance.

Counselling Keynotes

Be flexible, trust yourself, the person, the process — and trust God.

If someone is experiencing a difficulty in a relationship, or a physical symptom, consider inviting them to imagine that the person (or the headache, swollen joint or whatever) is in the opposite chair, and facilitate them as they conduct a dialogue with the person (symptom).

When working with ego-states, or facilitating decision making, it can be useful for the person to move to different chairs to express the thoughts and feelings each represents.

Putting Jesus 'in the chair' is a powerful technique which can prove very humbling, yet enriching.

1. Frederick S. Perls, *Gestalt Therapy Verbatim*, Bantam Books, New York, 1971.

2. Eric Berne, *Transactional Analysis in Psychotherapy*, Grove Press, New York, 1961.

3. Eric Berne, *Principles of Group Treatment*, Oxford University Press, Oxford, 1966.

4. Eric Berne, *Transactional Analysis in Psychotherapy*.

5. A. Lorean Roberts, *Transactional Analysis Approach to Counselling*, in the 'Guidance Monograph Series', Series VIII, Theories of Counselling and Psychotherapy, Houghton Mifflin, Boston, 1975.

6. Eric Berne, *Transactional Analysis in Psychotherapy*.

7. A. Lorean Roberts, *op. cit.*

8. John McNeel, *Transactional Analysis Journal*, Vol 6, No. 1, January 1976.

Part Two

4

THE WHOLE IS GREATER THAN
THE SUM OF THE PARTS

.

Increasing Awareness using Insights and Methods
from Gestalt Therapy

In the previous chapter I described chair work, which comes from
Gestalt therapy. Whether or not you had previously encountered chair
work, you will already have some experiential awareness of Gestalt
psychology, out of which Gestalt therapy grew.

Try this simple experiment:

Look at these stars

        *   *
        *   *
        *   *

Few people perceive them as a random collection of marks on the page.
Rather, most people perceive an arrangement of two columns of stars.
This illustrates a basic tenet of Gestalt psychology, which is that as human
beings we tend to perceive – and even impose – order and structure on
our environment. That is, we have an inner drive to close Gestalts. We
are moved, in other words, towards wholeness and completeness.

We are driven to close Gestalts in everyday life – to scratch when
we itch; eat when we are hungry; shed clothes when we are hot;

urinate when our bladders are full. Gestalt therapy takes this under-standing further, into the realm of our emotional functioning, and has as its focus our need to resolve issues which have not been completed to our satisfaction.

In Gestalt therapy great attention is paid to language – vocabulary, phraseology, tone of voice – as well as to non-verbal 'language', as these aspects of our behaviour often indicate the Gestalts which are currently pressing to be closed.

Gestalt therapy seeks to promote assimilation of new, maturing life experi-ences…through simply providing a context and stimulus for a person to experi-ment with 'being who he is'. He will change as a result of increased awareness of the choices he is in fact making all the time.[1]

Metaphor as a Literal Description of Experience

The wonderful richness of our language offers many choices of words and phrases. Exploration of these can be therapeutic by 'providing (just such) a context and stimulus'.[2] Counselling courses sometimes include an exercise in which students are invited to list as many refer-ences as they can to physical effects stemming from involvement with people or events, in order to increase their awareness of the way in which language mirrors experience. Typically, such lists include phras-es such as 'gets under my skin' or 'keeps me on my toes'. At first sight these may seem completely symbolic, but on closer inspection they can usually be seen to have a degree of literal truth, too. For example, being 'kept on one's toes' by a person or demand, contains a sense of increased alertness and preparedness – like a runner waiting for a race to start. Initially, it may seem too far-fetched to claim that saying someone 'gets under my skin' is describing a literal sensation. Yet the phrase refers to a sense of being intruded upon, invaded, of having one's very personhood infiltrated, which can very neatly be expressed as someone 'getting under my skin'.

Perls et al[3] offer this exercise:

An extremely useful method of grasping the meaning of particular aches or tensions is to call up appropriate expressions of popular speech. These invariably contain long-tested wisdom. For instance:

'I am stiff-necked; am I stubborn? I have a pain in the neck; what gives me a pain in the neck? I stretch my head high; am I haughty? I stick my chin out; am I leading with it? My brows arch; am I supercilious? I have a catch in my throat; do I want to cry? I am whistling in the dark; am I afraid of something? My flesh creeps; am I horrified? My brows beetle; am I full of rage? I feel swollen; am I ready to burst with anger? My throat is tight; is there something I can't swallow? My middle feels queasy; what can't I stomach?'[4]

By listening out for phrases of this kind we can learn more about a person's internal experience.

We can learn even more about a person's internal world by observing posture, movements and gestures. Sometimes this simply provides us with clues about the person, or pointers as to how best to work with them. At other times, we can serve people best by directing their attention to their bodies. For example, a person who sits slumped, saying in a barely audible voice 'I'm feeling all right really' is giving contradictory verbal and non-verbal messages. You could draw this to his attention by spelling out, 'You say you're feeling all right, yet I notice that your voice is quiet and you are hunched in your chair, and I wonder whether you *really* feel all right?' You may prefer to direct the person's attention more obliquely, in which case you could simply ask, 'How does your voice sound as you say that?' or 'Notice how you are sitting. Does it match what you just said?'

It has been said that the tongue can lie but the body cannot. People may be able to exercise sufficient control over their general posture to give a physical message which is congruent with their words, but be betrayed by a slight movement, particularly of their feet. A woman who wishes to be seen as forgiving and 'Christian' may say she bears no grudges towards her ex-husband – but accompany the words with a kicking movement. In this case the classic Gestalt intervention would be 'What is your foot saying?' No doubt you can find a way to draw attention to a non-verbal message of this kind which suits your counselling style.

(Incidentally, I recall setting out to make a gentle dig at this kind of approach, when I had first come across it, and was still unconvinced as to its value or validity. However, I got my comeuppance! A friend, whom I knew had come across Gestalt, had developed a rash on the back of her left hand. With heavy irony I asked 'Ah – and why is it *that* hand that's got the rash?' To my surprise, she answered without hesitation: 'Because that's my ugly hand. I don't like that one. The other one is beautiful.')

It is necessary to gauge a person's level of understanding before launching into questions such as 'What is your leg saying?' Each profession has its jargon, of course, but used in the wrong context, or prematurely, such words or phrases can be a hindrance to communication rather than a help. If I expect a person will be able to respond easily to a Gestalt approach, I may ask 'If your leg could talk, what would it be saying?' in place of the bald classic Gestalt question, 'What is your leg saying?' Sometimes this draws a blank, indicating that there is more 'unpacking' of the concept to do.

Simon demonstrated a huge split between his high achieving Adult self and his frightened Inner Child. I came to realize that he lacked the vocabulary with which to communicate his feelings, and even lacked the means of identifying them. I noticed that his stomach had rumbled in two or three consecutive sessions, but he had clapped his hand to his stomach and been content with purely physical explanations. I also noticed that he referred to it as his 'stomach *growling*'.

The next week, when I asked what it was saying, we went down the usual route of 'Nothing. It must be something I ate.' However, he had begun that session talking about a television programme in which a robot had said it was learning how to feel, which was a notion with which Simon identified. I talked to him about the possibility that he did not know the language of feelings. I also referred to something he had said earlier: that, when he is prayed for in church, he does not know when the Holy Spirit has come in greater power, though other people seem to know. I talked about his being able to learn to recognize those signs (warmth, tingling, fluttering eyelids, deep peace) and similarly being able to learn to recognize the signs of emotion.

Referring again to Simon's stomach growling I asked him 'When do animals growl?'

'To warn other animals off…as a threat…when they're hurt,' he replied.

'Might your stomach be warning me off?'

(Laughs) 'It's not very frightening?'

(Laughs) 'I don't feel very frightened…But might your stomach be feeling threatened?'

'It doesn't want people to get too close.'

'It sounds as if your stomach is saying it is frightened. You said animals growl when they are hurt. How is your stomach hurting?'

Suddenly it was as though the scales fell from Simon's eyes and he gained insight into what he had been doing to himself: 'I clench it!'

Simon then described memories from childhood of clenching his stomach against physical pain, then translating this into clenching against emotional pain. He connected it with clenching his stomach during ministry, as a way of keeping God at a distance. By this route we were able to explore Simon's transferred emotions from his violent father – who frequently beat Simon – onto God, from whom he expected punishment and retribution more than blessing and compassion.

Earlier in the same session we had explored the rapport between us and the wariness I sensed in Simon in certain circumstances. This work on his stomach 'growling' provided an ideal extension of that. In other circumstances it could have proved to be the *launch-pad* for such an explanation: revelations of process and the moment-by-moment relationship unfolding in the counselling room are two sides of the same coin. It is usually extremely profitable to make clear how they relate to each other.

Bringing Head and Heart Closer Together

Often, we disguise our internal experience – our real feelings – by covering them up with words. No doubt you have often heard someone describe a traumatic event, such as the death of someone they loved, in a way that betrays little emotion. In Gestalt parlance they would be described as 'coming from their head' and a therapist would probably encourage them to move instead to expressing their feelings or 'coming from their gut'.

Some people, especially those who have been in counselling for a while, and who are familiar with certain terms and concepts, can make this change simply in response to having the current state of affairs pointed out. Students on counselling courses, for example, or others who are practised at taking the client role, can usually move swiftly from being in their 'head' and get into their 'gut'.

For other people, though, a bridge is required to help them make the transition. This can often be erected by a sensitive response to the person's vocabulary and phraseology. Taking a key word or phrase and inviting the client to experience it more fully can have the effect of moving them from behind a defence built from words into a more open acknowledgement of the affective (feeling) component.

Returning to the earlier examples, the phrases relating to people being 'a pain in the neck' or having other physical effects on us could be repeated to the client, and he or she could be asked to experience the impact of that claim. The client could be urged to literally feel the weight of the burden imposed by the person, and to respond to that.

Giving Permission to Abandon 'Head' – Temporarily

I have spoken of a bridge which is often required to help people acknowledge and express their feelings. In fact, there is a sense in which *two* bridges are needed. The other is a general bridge which affirms their ability to think, evaluate, rationalize and compute. Early Gestalt practitioners down-played the value of the intellectual processes to a degree which I find unacceptable.

An oft-quoted injunction of Fritz Perls is 'lose your mind and come to your senses'.[5] Parlett and Page write:

The legacy from this era has been that Gestalt therapy has sometimes been abused, practised in an overly confrontative way, and regarded as anti-intellectual. In the last ten years there has been a re-evaluation of these attitudes and a wholesale change back towards the original fundamental ideas...[6]

We all need to be able to think logically and weigh up options and so forth. The limitations imposed on people with mental handicaps, senile dementia and some psychiatric conditions by their difficulties in these areas is surely evidence for this. To decry the importance of such abilities is, in my opinion, folly. However, there are undoubtedly times in counselling, when colluding with someone who is staying firmly in the intellectual realm is not therapeutic. In this case, intellectualizing is being used as a defence and the feelings related to the topic are being masked. In instances of this kind the therapist's role is to help the person discover, acknowledge, express and own their feelings and projections.

Projection: Psychological and Therapeutic Processes

To understand the psychological process of projection it is helpful to compare it with the projection of visual images onto a screen. The screen is blank but becomes coloured by what is sent by the projector. We make projections all the time; that is, we perceive our environment (including the other people in it) according to the attributes we 'put in'.

I recall hearing a story during a school assembly many years ago which illustrated this principle. A man was on his way to a distant town and met a visitor who was returning from that town. The traveller asked him what kind of people lived there and received an answer full of negative terms such as 'mean', 'surly' and 'violent'. He carried on travelling and met another visitor returning from the same town. Upon asking *his* opinion of the inhabitants the man received a glowing report of people who were 'sunny natured', 'helpful' and 'honest'. The point which was then drawn out was that, as the two visitors were speaking about the same group of people, their judgements were coloured by their own attributes. Therapeutically, projections can be explored in order to foster self-awareness and, if desired, provide the impetus for change. My work with Lara, in the following case study, provides an example of this.

Often, working with clients involves exploring aspects of their relationships with others. It can be releasing for them to learn that, when we have strong feelings about a person (whether positive or negative) it is often due to the strength of our projections. For example, you dislike someone whom you regard as mean – where is your own meanness? Or you greatly admire someone whom you perceive as confident – what are you doing with your own confidence?

Chair work or 'I am (the person)' can help people re-own these projections. By reversing roles with someone we see as different from us we can discover their viewpoint, which frequently increases our tolerance and compassion. In the second case study Jemma uses two images, which turn out to represent herself and another person. In this piece of work she clarifies her opinion of, and attitude towards, herself and the other woman.

Case Study 1

Lara: Exploring a Powerful Image

Until a boating accident left her with a partial disability, Lara's future had looked very promising. She was completing her training as a teacher, specializing in sports, and was a well-known figure in amateur athletics. All this had ended abruptly as the neurological damage she had sustained caused problems not only in the areas of her mobility and fine motor skills, but also in her ability to communicate.

Counselling sessions had provided a vehicle for Lara to consider and re-evaluate her attitudes and relationships. She had explored her changed expectations for her life (especially her career and sporting interests), and the concomitant reduction in self-esteem. The process involved a certain amount of recalling the past, some aspects of which she had faced with regret.

At the end of one session, Lara indicated the shorts she was wearing, made from a pair of cut-down jeans.

'When I opened the wardrobe this morning I saw these hanging there. These were the "accident jeans" and Mum often tells me to throw them away. Where my leg was broken, they'd got a long worn patch. But they were my favourite garment and I didn't want to throw them away. Anyway, I don't remember anything about the accident. [Lara is referring to her own lack of negative associations between the jeans and the accident, contrasted with her mother's strong associations between them.] So this morning I decided to cut them down.'

Lara's manner in mentioning this decision alerted me to the fact that this carried considerable import and I invited her to speak as if she were the cut-down jeans:

'I've been cut down in my prime. I was useful and I still can be, but in a different way. I was marked but now I'm not.'

The power and precision of projective techniques never ceases to amaze me. In three sentences, Lara had summed up her current state and her reaction to it and had confirmed the impact of the previous session and its status as a life-changing moment.

We sat in silence for a minute or so, while Lara considered the statements she had just made. Then she went on quietly:

'The accident *did* mean I was cut down in my prime. But that needn't mean that my useful life has come to an end. And I *was* marked – but not any more.'

There was no time to unpack the symbol of the jeans any further, so I suggested to Lara that she may like to work with the symbol on her own. Some people draw, paint or even sculpt an image which seems particularly forceful. I suggested to Lara that she could sketch the jeans in their various states (unblemished, marked and cut-down) and perhaps add the words and phrases which came to mind as she sketched.

As well as listening out for key words or phrases which crop up naturally, and seem to jump out at us, clamouring for their full impact to be recognized, there are other images which come only at our invitation, but which can prove to be equally powerfully therapeutic. In the case study that follows, the crucial image and descriptive phrases came up when I followed a hunch and asked some specific, direct questions. The manner in which they appear is less important than that the person is facilitated in exploring their projected responses to the image.

Case Study 2

Jemma: Identifying a Vital Image
'I am a...'

Jemma's self-esteem had taken a nose dive and she doubted if it would ever creep back upwards. She had recognized for over a year that her husband was tense and unlike his usual self, but had put this down to anxieties related to his work. Discovering the true cause of his remote manner with her came as an immense shock. Not only was he in an adulterous relationship, but Jemma had been horrified to discover that the 'other woman' was one of several 'massage girls' her husband had visited.

By the time Jemma came to me her husband had ended the affair and they were living in an uneasy truce. We had worked for a few weeks on aspects of her attitudes and behaviour and I had developed a strong sense of her having marginalized her sexuality. Acting on a hunch I asked her to describe her bedroom.

(I sometimes remind students on counselling courses that clients have few pre-conceived ideas about what goes on in counselling. Clients also desperately want the process to 'work'. Taken together, these factors combine to mean that they will usually go along with just about anything the counsellor asks. This is one reason why the counsellor–client relationship needs such clear boundaries: the potential for exploitation and abuse is so great. On the other hand, when the counsellor's motives and ethics are good, a client's compliance also eases the way for a counsellor who is making interventions, which, in other settings, would be considered bizarre. As I point out to students, the power which the counsellor holds is phenomenal. If she were to ask clients to hang upside down from the light fitting, many would be likely to do their best to comply.)

Only fazed for a moment, Jemma began the description I had asked for and my suspicion was borne out. The house turned out to be a T-shaped building, with the main bedroom at the bottom of the single storey stem. A bathroom and guest room made up the rest of the stem. By contrast, the living areas, another bathroom and the children's bedrooms were on the (two storey) crosspiece of the T. It then came as no surprise to hear that Jemma and her husband had designed the house but that he had wanted their bedroom in a different position.

I felt that Jemma's description of the layout of her house confirmed – if only tangentially – my impression of her having pushed acknowledgement of her sexuality to the periphery of her life. She then went on to describe the bedroom. The bed turned out to be a four-poster, with a white lacy frilly net canopy and dark-stained poles.

One important notion from Gestalt is that of acknowledging the existence within oneself of both 'polarities' of a quality. Jemma's description of her bed with its lacy (feminine) canopy and stark (masculine) poles seemed to lend itself to an exploration of these polarities, so I invited Jemma to speak as if she were the bed.

(Some counsellors begin as bluntly as this, but I prefer to let the person know that I realize that my instruction is probably unexpected and may well sound outlandish. I sometimes pre-empt any protestations by clients that they feel 'silly' or 'embarrassed' by saying that most people feel foolish when they begin using this technique, but soon get used to doing it, and eventually find it useful.)

As Gestalt therapy concentrates heavily on the 'here and now', it is important to encourage the person to speak in the present tense and in the first person. Jemma began by saying, 'The bed is...' and I immediately interjected 'I am...' to help her make the necessary shift.

After one or two false starts, she began to speak in the present tense and in the first person: 'I am the bed...' Immediately, she started describing herself in positive terms such as 'unique', 'special', 'superior', 'beautiful', 'a work of art'. She then described a little of her history from which it emerged that the bed had been handmade by her husband, who had previously made another, smaller one. A new, unexpected set of polarities was soon in evidence.

An important notion in Gestalt is that of 'figure and ground', which refers to the idea that a figure in a picture is seen against some kind of background. Taking the example of an actual picture, you may initially look only at the main object (the 'figure'). However, on closer examination you may find that in addition to the person, animal, house or other object in the foreground, there exists a backdrop (or 'ground') which has features of its own. Gestalt therapy focuses not only on the problem or image a person reports (the figure) but also on bringing its context (the ground) into awareness.

Here, the first bed existed as 'figure', while the second bed formed the vital 'ground'. Both needed to be brought into awareness. Jemma's statements as this second bed were extremely telling. This bed represented the woman with whom her husband had had an affair. It was smaller than Jemma (less important); had previously been 'made' by him (double entendre); and was described by Jemma as 'inferior' and 'not as good as me in any way'. What is more, this other bed had 'broken when too many people bounced on it' (another double entendre). The contrasts between herself and 'the other woman' were clear and indicated that her self-esteem, although severely dented, was actually more positive than it had seemed. Her attitude to the 'other' bed revealed that she considered herself vastly superior to the smaller, cheaper version which had collapsed through over-use.

Jemma had had no previous experience of projective techniques. When I asked, at the end of her descriptions of the two beds, whether the main four-poster bed could represent her she looked taken aback. She then quickly pointed out the projected identity of the other bed, and points of similarity between each bed and the person it represented. For example, the 'massage girl' was extremely thin and in poor health – perhaps because of the combination of life style and promiscuity. Jemma did not consider her a threat and felt that she herself had very much more to offer her husband.

It was also helpful for us to examine the contrasts, or 'polarities', *within* her description of the main four-poster bed. Her

husband had built the bed and she had 'dressed' it, and she agreed
with my suggestion that symbolically the white lace and the dark
poles might echo, respectively, his desire for passion and hers for
intimacy (or 'sex' and 'lovemaking' as she distinguished them).

Jemma's work included a number of polarities: the two beds
were old/new; superior/inferior; expensive/cheap; well-made/
broken down; full-size/small. During that session it seemed
right to limit the work done on her projections onto the beds to
those contrasting herself with the 'other woman'. Often,
though, the most productive personal growth work comes from
re-owning even the projections relating to things and people outside of ourselves as representing some parts of us. Thus, I could
have invited Jemma to explore those aspects of herself which she
experiences as inferior, small, broken-down, cheap or old. By so
doing, her compassion for her husband's mistress would probably
have further increased. (As it was, she grew considerably in forgiveness of her, and empathy with her by speaking as one bed
describing the other.)

The key points, then, from this account of one session with Jemma, are
as follows:

- We had sufficient rapport for me to follow a hunch and ask her to
  describe the layout of her house.
- Her description of her bed sounded as if it contained symbolic
  material; it was 'figural', so I encouraged her to remain focussed
  on the bed.
- Polarities are important in Gestalt therapy and are useful to help
  people re-own aspects of themselves or their situation which they
  had buried.
- It is important to find a way to introduce Gestalt approaches
  which feels comfortable for you. Clients invariably report feeling
  foolish when first trying them. If you, too, feel awkward this will
  compound their unease.
- Encouraging a person to speak in the present tense and first
  person is important and sometimes requires some modelling by
  the counsellor.

• Hearing herself give voice to her projections increased Jemma's confidence in her own qualities. The images of the two beds only emerged as we worked. By contrast, a fruitful simile or metaphor is sometimes spontaneously expressed – handed to the counsellor on a plate, as it were. For example, a man may say, 'I'm all at sea.' It could be enlightening for him to speak as 'the sea', as it may help him acknowledge more fully than before his sense of helplessness and of being at the mercy of huge, unstoppable forces.

Personal Metaphor in the Bible

Methods used in Gestalt evolved in part from the work of Carl Gustav Jung.[7] He used what he called 'Active Imagination' as a means of capturing, furthering and integrating thoughts and emotions. But the idea of using symbols to concretize inner processes did not begin with him, of course, and the scriptures are full of examples. Here I concentrate on some biblical instances of simile and metaphor focussed on people.

Feeling Your Way into Scripture

Scripture abounds with references to groups of people cast in illustrative terms. As you read familiar passages from the Bible you may find that your appreciation increases if you deliberately allow yourself to enter into these illustrations. Some years ago I attended a talk given by a very frail elderly lady (who died not long after). A prime example of someone whose physical self may have been ailing, but whose spirit was sharp, she opened the eyes of those present to the wonderful truth of our identity as fellow heirs with Christ. She so convinced us of our identity as princesses that we could almost feel the weight of our crowns!

In his writings, St Paul writes of Christians as runners (1 Corinthians 9:24–27) and soldiers (Ephesians 6: 10–17). These passages and their applications are so familiar yet we can perhaps draw still more from them if we spend some time feeling our way into the actual identity of an athlete or an armoured fighter.

We have seen the usefulness of placing oneself in any image which seems particularly important, and of switching to become some other part of the context. Many passages of scripture lend themselves beautifully to this 'figure and ground' approach. In Gestalt therapy the phrase 'I am a...' often occurs when a person explores aspects of his or her personality. For example, a person may be struck (in a dream, meditation or poem) by an image such as a rose. In addition to working with the meaning which the rose has for her, she could also be encouraged to 'be' the soil in which the rose is growing, the gardener who planted it, or the vase in which it is now displayed. For Christians, the obvious echo is the series of proclamations made by Jesus and recorded in St John's Gospel, each beginning 'I am...'. We can use the figure and ground notion and find how we are represented as a consequence of each of these 'Great I Am's. 'I am the Good Shepherd' (John 10:11), for example, leads directly to our being the sheep. The statements: 'I am the Bread of Life' (John 6:35) and 'I am the Light of the World' (John 8:12) cast us as starving people and those in darkness respectively. Each such 'figure' necessarily produces its associated 'ground'.

You may care to experience scripture in a different way from usual, and at the same time appreciate some of the potential of the projective approach, by taking yourself fully into one of these examples of 'ground'. Aim to enter as completely as possible into the truth of being a sheep, or a starving person, or someone in darkness:

What does your body feel like? What can you see? What can you hear?

Don't ignore your other senses:

What can you smell and taste? Where are you? What are your surroundings like?

Speak as that person: 'I am a...', and get the fullest sense you can of your total being as that person.

When you have rooted yourself in this identity, let Jesus – as the Good Shepherd, or Bread of Life or Light of the World – come to you. How do you feel towards the shepherd, bread or light? Again, check with each of your senses – what does the shepherd, bread or light look, sound, feel, smell and taste like? What difference does its coming make to you? How do you respond?

The next stage is to put yourself in the role of the 'figure' you have chosen – shepherd, bread or light – and again enter into that experience, just as fully as you became the 'ground'.

Notice how you feel to be coming to the sheep, or to the hungry or benighted person. Focus your experience by speaking, beginning for example 'I am the Good Shepherd' and relating how you feel towards the sheep.

As you experience each role you may find yourself flooded with new awarenesses. Taking the perspective of Jesus – whether as Good Shepherd, Bread of Life or whatever – may have enabled you to feel more fully than ever before His compassion and mercy. And you may have been able to acknowledge at a deeper level than previously the utter dependence of yourself as sheep, starving person or person in darkness.

Using Scripture as a Starting Point

In a series on cheerful giving in 1990, in the Bible reading notes *Alive to God*,[8] the following words appeared:

Today we read Psalm 23. David, who had been a shepherd, chose this image to describe God's love and care. Is there a special image that you would choose? 'The Lord is my...'

Here, the writers are recommending using scripture as a jumping-off point and allowing the Holy Spirit to prompt into awareness a personally appropriate metaphor.

Why not consider that psalm now? You may like to use the concept of parent (or, specifically, mother or father) and meditate along these lines:

The Lord is my parent (or mother, or father),
I shall be given everything I need.
She (He) nestles me against her (his) warm body,
Gives me comforting milk to drink,
And soothes my fractiousness.

(Rewritten in this way the psalm takes on more than a passing resemblance to Psalm 131.)

Having revelled in the sensation of receiving such loving care, you may like to imagine yourself as God, the loving parent nurturing you as a baby.

The notion of the parenthood of God can be hard for many people to relate to, and an exercise such as this can go some way towards helping them to appreciate the tender, nurturing heart of God. It may be, though, that another image altogether is more personally meaningful for you; there are many possibilities, of course. Should you return to the experience at a later date, you may easily find yourself working with a different image on that occasion.

Conclusion

Gestalt therapy is a complex discipline. Becoming qualified requires a good deal of time and commitment, yet some of the insights can be useful tools for many counsellors. Elsewhere I will discuss the Gestalt approach to dreamwork and guided fantasies. However, for more detail about Gestalt therapy I suggest you consult some of the many available books. Better still, since Gestalt is above all things an experiential discipline, join a group or consult a Gestalt therapist!

Counselling Keynotes

Listen out for key words and phrases. Repeat them, or ask clients to do so. Facilitate clients in increasing their experience of the impact of these words or phrases and of the full meaning which they have for them.

Recognize projections in people's speech. Help clients re-own these by inviting them to speak as the object concerned. Be firm about people staying in the first person and in the present tense as they do this.

Be aware of the context in which concepts arise — the so-called 'figure and ground'. Bring the ground into awareness, too.

Remember to pay attention to non-verbal behaviour, as well as to speech. Ask your own variation on 'what is your foot (or fist or neck or whatever) saying?'

1. Michael Parlett and Faye Page, *Gestalt Therapy, A Handbook*, Open University Press, Milton Keynes, 1990, p. 184.

2. Michael Parlett and Faye Page, *op. cit.*

3. Frederick Perls, Ralph F. Hefferline and Paul Goodman, *Gestalt Therapy, Excitement and Growth in the Human Personality*, Souvenir Press, 1951.

4. Frederick Perls, Ralph F. Hefferline and Paul Goodman, *op. cit.*, p. 165.

5. Quoted in Petruska Clarkson, *Gestalt Counselling in Action*, Sage, 1989.

6. Michael Parlett and Faye Page, *op. cit.*

7. Carl G. Jung (ed.), *Man and His Symbols*, Aldus Books Ltd, 1964.

8. Judith Allford and Graham Jones, *Alive to God*, from 'Cheerful Giving' series, 20 May 1990.

PICTURE THIS...

Visualization and Imagery

The importance of imagery in scripture has already been made clear. The Bible was written to engage our mind and spirit, and to reach us via our inward being. Therefore the Bible is written for the right side of our brains, as well as for the left – it is written in the language of logic and rationality, and also of creativity and poetry.

St Ignatius of Loyola (1491–1556)[1] recognized that the Bible addresses the whole person, and suggested the use of five methods in his Spiritual Exercises. Designed to take us more deeply into scripture, and to enable us to commune with God at a more profound level, the Ignatian Spiritual Exercises represent a means of making a whole-person response to passages from the Bible.

One of his methods involves taking an event from Christ's life and applying to it each of the five senses: sight, hearing, smell, taste and touch. Another of his methods involves meditating on a passage of scripture and asking to know, love and follow the Lord. Memory, will and understanding are then brought to bear, to facilitate the identifying of some action or decision to be taken.

The proliferation of various personal growth activities in the 1970s resulted in an expansion of meditative techniques. They were used in personal growth groups; taught as techniques for overcoming stress and fighting cancer; and used by New Age followers to make contact with their spirit guides.

The enthusiastic use by New Agers of visualization and guided fantasies led some Christians to shun the techniques. In my opinion this is an example of throwing out the baby with the bathwater, and – even worse – of allowing things which have enriched the Christian tradition for centuries to be hijacked by another group. We have become suspicious of something which, through many previous centuries, was regarded as normal, mainstream Christian practice. I feel strongly that Christians lose much of the essential richness, texture and vibrancy of their faith if it is reduced to a two-dimensional, pursed lipped, left side of the brain experience.

Therapeutically, the possible range of applications of visualization techniques is wide. The most obvious examples are inviting a person to 'enter into' a passage of scripture (Ignatian style); guided fantasy (from a book, cultural myths or the therapist's imagination); guided imaginative prayer, for example 'seeing' and 'feeling' Jesus come and talk to us or cradle us; an idiosyncratic image, for example, from a person's speech or dream life; and working with an image given by the Holy Spirit as a 'picture' or 'word of knowledge'.

'Entering Into' Scripture (Ignatian Style)

The power of the Word of God to bring transformation should not be underestimated. Books such as Joyce Huggett's *Open to God*[2] or Mary Zimmer's *Sister Images*,[3] contain a variety of meditations and 'imaginative contemplations' which open up the scriptures to us in profound, often very moving ways. No doubt any Christian who regularly reads the Bible has experienced moments of intense identification with a biblical character. If we are suffering we may 'meet' ourselves in one of the psalms, or, if feeling blamed for our own predicament, we may find that Job's words closely echo our own experience. Or, impatient for God to act we may try to force his hand – and see our actions mirrored by those of Abraham sleeping with Hagar (Genesis 16:1–4). Our style in approaching God may be like that of the woman with the haemorrhage who came quietly (Luke 8:43–4) or of the centurion who brought reasoning to bear (Luke 7:6–8) or even like Bartimaeus whose shouts drew Jesus' attention (Luke 18:35–43).

In working with clients, a passage of scripture which is well chosen (or, even better, prompted by the Holy Spirit) and offered at an appropriate time can function to break through destructive patterns of thought or behaviour.

Kenneth, a lay preacher, had come into counselling because his wife was threatening to leave him. As he explored his attitudes towards women in general and his wife in particular, he faced memories of an episode of 30 years earlier, when he was in his late teens and had acted in an inappropriately sexual way towards a girl of 10 whom he was looking after one evening. Until that moment he had denied to himself the gravity of what he had done.

Slowly Kenneth dismantled the wall of denial he had built. In labelling his behaviour as abusive, he recognized that the potential for the child to have suffered emotional damage was considerable, and that he had betrayed the trust of the whole family. In appreciating the true nature of what he had done, he was brought face to face with its sinfulness, both as an action and as indicating exploitative attitudes towards someone whom he had a responsibility to protect.

Counselling is a many-layered activity and we spent several sessions addressing the cognitive and emotional layers. This helped Kenneth understand the background to his dysfunctional attitudes and this isolated incident; mourn for himself as a child and for the girl whom he had exploited, and choose to adopt different standards of attitudes and behaviour. Incorporating these denied facts about himself and working with the issues to bring about resolution caused a great deal of heartache for Kenneth and he wondered whether he would ever feel reinstated by God to a place of acceptance.

It was at that point that I introduced the story of the Prodigal Son (Luke 15:11–32). I asked if he would like me to read it to him, and he agreed. Before I did so I spent a few moments reminding him of the cultural signs of the ring, denoting position and acceptance (mark of authority); robe (sign of distinction); sandals (slaves went barefoot); and fatted calf (for a special occasion) given to the son. I suggested that Kenneth get comfortable, close his eyes and relax his body and mind. I asked him to notice his breathing and then directed his attention to each part of his body in turn, allowing tension to be released from it.

Matching my pace to his slowed breathing, I then began to read the passage, suggesting first that he allow himself to enter into it as though he were the Prodigal Son.

Kenneth found this an extremely moving experience. As I read about the father running out to meet the son, he began to weep. His weeping had turned to sobs by the time I read that the father had commanded that the fatted calf be killed for this, his errant, 'no good' son. I suggested that Kenneth feel for himself the forgiveness, acceptance and love offered by God to him, just as the father was reconciled to the Prodigal Son. Kenneth afterwards reported that he had a strong sense of God embracing him and offering full restoration. In Kenneth's case the story ended there: he was no longer in touch with the family concerned so could not offer apologies to the young woman whom he had abused, nor to her family. Had this not been so, it would have been appropriate for us to consider such an action, following which he may have decided to seek forgiveness from them, as well as from God.

Guided Fantasy

In individual as well as group settings, guided fantasies can prove invaluable for helping people to explore and strengthen parts of themselves. In fact, 'guided fantasy' is a term I dislike, on the grounds that it seems to belittle what is often a profound psychological experience in which elements of the personality can be restructured. However the alternative, 'visualization', seems to me even more limited. The point about an experience of this kind is that it does not engage only one inner sense, but, in the imagination, is a whole body – indeed, it is a whole *person* experience. The self-help and therapeutic literature abound with examples and some particular guided fantasies have become well-known in therapeutic circles through frequent use. Most published examples have a strong projective element, containing references to objects designed to represent some specific part of the personality, such as streams (spirituality), concave objects (such as a cup or a cave: the feminine side), or subpersonalities (for example, a wise person). Others emphasize the Transactional

Analysis ego-states, for example, enabling the person to meet, befriend and nurture their own Inner Child.

Guided Imaginative Prayer

One way to move a person towards greater wholeness or to bring healing in specific areas of life is through guided imaginative prayer.

This form of healing, often known as 'healing of the memories' can be undertaken as an activity in its own right, as it were. Indeed, it is often used by those with no counselling training. On the other hand, it can emerge as an obvious next step in a therapeutic relationship, perhaps arising in the context of some Gestalt work. As Jesus is outside time, one asks Jesus to go back in time to the particular event which is troubling a person, and to bring healing.

One example I have witnessed was that of Jesus letting a man whose father was a DIY enthusiast – and very sarcastic of his son's early attempts to 'help' – assist him in some elementary carpentry and encouraging his efforts. Another was Jesus coming and lying between a woman and her rapist father – so that He, not she, suffered the abuse. Relatively often, and usually in group work, profound healing takes place when people re-experience their birth and sense Jesus welcoming them into the world with joy and excitement.

Sometimes, healing of the memories proceeds smoothly and beautifully without any hitch, but this is not always so. Then, other steps may need to be inserted or substituted. For example, some women who have been sexually abused find it too traumatic to picture Jesus in the scene as His maleness is experienced as compounding the threat and terror of the situation. Somewhat stumped when this first happened, I was then taken aback to hear the Pentecostal woman I was counselling announce, 'Mary has just come into the room. She's cradling me and carrying me away from him.' I had to think quickly to realize that in this woman's imaginative prayer, the Virgin Mary (on whom she had previously placed little emphasis) had come to remove her from her abuser.

There are also times when the person's Nurturing Parent or Adult needs to be engaged, to talk to the Child about Jesus. If a person's upbringing was very definitely outside the Church then his or her Child may need to be evangelized. It is not that the person is not fully saved, just that the emotional self sometimes lags behind the spiritual self and may require help in 'catching up'. This may be what is needed if a person says, in Child, 'I don't know who Jesus is' during regressive work of this kind.

Guided imaginative prayer can also be used to move a person on in their journey towards wholeness, without focussing on any specific past event. Asking where Jesus is, in the room right now, and encouraging the person to talk to Him is one form of such prayer. Another is a relaxation exercise, followed by a guided meditation on a theme such as being a sheep. (Are you inside the sheepfold or outside? Where is the shepherd?) It can be particularly powerful to invite Jesus into the person's current everyday life: I can recall being overwhelmed to find Him in my kitchen, doing the washing up! Open questions such as 'Is there anything Jesus wants to show you/tell you?' or 'Is there anywhere He wants to take you?' tend to enlarge the experience, rather than a more closed approach such as 'Jesus is holding out His arms. He wants to hug you.' Trust the Holy Spirit and the person's own insights.

Guided imaginative prayer sometimes emerges as a useful endeavour in the context of other therapeutic work. In a 'tight spot' it is not uncommon for people without much in the way of Christian understanding, let alone belief, to call out to God. So, for example, a person may be working on a theme – from a dream, perhaps – in which she is being mercilessly pursued. Asked whether there is anyone who could come and help, she may say 'God' or 'Jesus'. On the other hand she may say, 'A knight on a white charger' or 'a tiger'. Whatever her response, the next step is to suggest that she imagines the person or creature in the scene. If a dialogue ensues, and the chosen person is God or Jesus then, by definition, the conversation is a form of prayer. If the chosen person is not God or Jesus the image should still be honoured.

Visions and Words of Knowledge

Sometimes the Holy Spirit reveals the appropriate content for guided imagery. Not surprisingly, when this happens the results tend to be particularly profound and far-reaching.

One woman with whom I was working had suffered severe neglect in childhood. She mentioned during one session that she had read an account in a book on healing which included a reference to 'freeing the imprisoned spirit'. Reading this account put into perspective a series of visions which she had been given by God over the course of a week, in which just this seemed to have been achieved.

We agreed to focus on the series of 'pictures' and asked the Holy Spirit to direct our thoughts, words and imagination, and to achieve all that the Lord desired for that session. (Working through the pictures took a total of two sessions.) Having visualized the events when the pictures first came to her, Helen was now able to experience them more fully and to glean from them the healing which God intended.

Briefly, in the two sessions we 'fleshed out' the pictures, with the following outcome:

Helen first saw herself in a corridor, reluctant to open a door and confront what was inside. Jesus was there and gradually, with His compassionate presence, she became able to do so, and walked along the corridor and opened the door. At first she could see nothing, then her eyes became accustomed to the dark and she saw a small frightened, tear-stained girl huddled in one corner. Jesus went ahead of Helen and picked up the little girl, who was emaciated and dirty. As He did so, her skin became pink and plumper. He took her out of the room and out of the house. There, He gave her to Helen. As she took the child, she absorbed her into herself.

The following week, we worked with the second part. In this, Jesus and Helen were standing outside the same front door. Ahead was a beautiful garden, but reaching it entailed crossing a dark area. At the end of the first session Helen had reached this point and was reluctant to go any further. She realized that to do so would involve growing up, and did not yet feel ready for that.

However, at the second session Helen asked to continue where we had left off, but this time found that the transitional area was not so dark. She took Jesus' hand and they crossed together. He unlocked the gate and she went in eagerly. He watched with pleasure while she danced and skipped. He hugged her and she danced some more. Then the 'child' figure grew to teenage and finally to adulthood. At the end, Jesus held them both and Helen absorbed her younger part into herself.

Taken together, these sessions proved very powerful for Helen. We discussed what had happened from both a spiritual and psychological perspective – that is, freeing her imprisoned spirit and mending the split in her personality. These processes were pivotal for her healing: after these two sessions she discovered a new love for the Lord, and seemed to undergo a dramatic burst of increasing spiritual maturity.

Pursuing an Idiosyncratic Image

A Gestalt practitioner may pursue a great many of the word pictures and other images conjured up by clients. Most other therapists do so less often, but it can certainly be extremely helpful to pick up on some images, and invite people to explore them experientially.

These images may jump out at us as obvious 'figures' against the 'ground' of the rest of the content. Or we may become aware of them more slowly, perhaps when we notice them recurring in a person's speech. Sometimes a person will specifically draw our attention to an image and state that this is their desired focus for the session.

When I was working with Louise, a young woman in her twenties who came into counselling for help with depression, symbols were plentiful. She is a strong visualizer, so clear images often occurred in her speech.

A keen amateur artist, she had responded eagerly to my suggestion, at the end of one session, that she find some way to record her thoughts and feelings. I had explained that some people like to keep a written journal, while others find a series of pictures more to their liking. Louise brought a detailed picture to the next session, and we spent the time 'unpacking' the many images, which included the sun, a cross, a baby in the womb, a single flower, tears on a sad face, darkness and a candle.

Louise came for a session shortly afterwards, bringing the words of a secular song which she had heard that week and which she had found meaningful. I read them and agreed with her opinion that they could be heard as Jesus expressing his love for us. The song featured the same polarities of despair and rescue, neglect and nurture as had appeared in the picture and I asked her to consider the song and picture side by side. She pointed out that they embraced similar themes and I asked her which image from the picture seemed to stand out most. 'The baby,' she answered, indicating a baby in its mother's womb. I invited her to speak as the baby and she said she was 'warm and secure, needing attention and growing slowly'. I then suggested she speak as the mother, in whose womb the baby was depicted. Louise spoke of loving and caring for the baby and providing for all its needs.

Among the many objects which I keep in my consulting room are several miniature human figures. I selected a tiny baby doll (about a centimetre long) and put it in her hand. She gazed at it and I asked what the baby needed. 'Cotton wool,' she replied immediately. It so happened that, in my basket of bits and pieces I have a small piece of cotton wool so I unearthed it and she then cradled the baby doll, in cotton wool, in her palm. While she did so I read:

Can a mother forget the baby at her breast and have no compassion on the child she has borne? Though she may forget, I will not forget you! See, I have engraved you on the palms of my hands.

ISAIAH 49:15, 16A

As I had made an obvious connection between the protective figure and God, I invited her to move to another chair and in her imagination to look back at herself holding the doll, representing Jesus holding her. After a few moments I suggested she return to her original chair, consciously moving into the Lord's embrace. She did so, and sat quietly for a while with her eyes closed.

When she fully opened her eyes I was amazed to hear her say 'The Lord came and sang the song to me, but this time it had different words.' She wrote the new verse down, then I read:

The Lord your God is with you, he is mighty to save. He will take great delight in you, he will quiet you with his love, he will rejoice over you with singing.

ZEPHANIAH 3:17

Finally, I invited her to sing the new verse to the little doll in its cotton wool in the palm of her hand. Hearing this was extraordinary as the style and theme mirrored and developed the original song.

The session with Louise highlights a number of important principles in counselling.

- Clients often develop just a few basic themes over the weeks or months in which they are being counselled. These may appear in various guises at different times, but it is helpful for the clients' sense of wholeness to have links made between them as they recur. By inviting Louise to place the picture and song side by side I allowed her to perceive these links for herself.
- It is good practice to notice polarities and to encourage clients to express both sides; hence, after she had made reference to the baby's dependency, I encouraged her to explore the role of the one on whom the baby depends.
- Using actual objects (or pictures, for example) roots a person's experience in concrete reality. By working with *both* the depicted baby *and* the baby doll, Louise's dependency on God was doubly reinforced.
- In counselling Christians, scripture provides the bedrock against which everything can be judged, and on which everything can be built. It is often there as common ground between us and sometimes it is right to remind clients of particular verses.
- By asking Louise to move to a different physical position, I invited her to 'take a step back' and thereby gain a different perspective.

Often a useful technique, here it allowed her to see herself
nestling in the Lord's protective grasp.

- Taking this 'step backwards' is as valid as her previous experience
of feeling her dependency 'from the inside'; hence my suggestion
that, as she returned to her chair, she should blend into the image
she had been seeing.

- It is beautiful when the Holy Spirit joins our endeavours and adds
a new dimension. By giving Louise another verse for the song,
He validated her and our work together – and continued the
multi-modal technique which I had been using! This was one of
those moments in counselling where I was rendered speechless
and dewy-eyed!

- Inviting Louise to repeat the song performed a dual function, of
reinforcing what the Lord had said, and encouraging her to carry
out some nurturing of herself. (Working with people who have
received inadequate parenting, one can help them provide for
their own vulnerable selves – their Child part, in TA terminology
– the nurturing which they would have liked their parents to give.
Used in that way, it is known as 'self reparenting'.)

Counselling Keynotes

*In working with any kind of guided imagery it is important to go slowly. The
person will have shifted gear and be functioning at a slightly different state of
consciousness. Notably, right side of brain functions will predominate. Remember
that the right side of the brain is not normally used for verbal processes.*

*Take account of the person's ego-state and adjust your language (vocabulary
and syntax) accordingly. In particular, speak slowly and simply when a person
is in Child. This is even more crucial if a person regresses, and begins to oper-
ate as if he or she were a child.*

*Especially when using biblical material, or specifically Christian guided
imagery, allow plenty of room for the Holy Spirit. If you can hold off long
enough from saying something like 'Now let Jesus come towards you and hug
you' you will almost certainly be moved and delighted to find that He does
something even more nurturing. (One woman, who as a child had always been*

dressed in clean but ill-matching clothes, was very touched to find Jesus giving her Child part an outfit in just the right colour and style; admiring her and then hugging her.)

Take your cues from the person. My client, Helen, found herself blocked at the end of one session and did not want to go further. I immediately brought the imagery to a close. The following week Helen asked to continue and was able to bring the work to a beautiful resolution.

Always remember that techniques which rely mainly on the right side of the brain are very powerful. My aim in this book is not to suggest ways in which an untrained person may 'dabble' but to extend the skills of those who have already undergone some training. A vital rule of thumb is never use a method on someone else which you have not experienced for yourself.

Allow plenty of time for people to re-establish themselves in 'real time' as it were. After work of this kind, people sometimes need help in re-orienting themselves. Should a person seem to be 'not quite with you', have them direct their attention to current reality. I sometimes ask people to state brief biographical details, describe their clothing, count the number of windows in the room or (in a group situation) look at each person in the room in turn and engage briefly with them. Always spend time checking that psychologically a person is fully back in the room with you — not still three years old and dancing in a cornfield! This is of crucial importance if the person has to drive home and I sometimes suggest they take a walk or sit in the car for a while before attempting to drive.

On a few occasions I have offered people a cup of tea before sending them on their way, in order to be sure that they really were back in current reality.

1. St Ignatius of Loyola, *Spiritual Exercises*, Hodder & Stoughton, London, 1989.

2. Joyce Huggett, *Open to God*, Hodder & Stoughton, London, 1989.

3. Mary Zimmer, *Sister Images, Guided Meditations from the Stories of Biblical Women*, Abingdon Press, Nashville, 1993.

6

WORTH A THOUSAND WORDS?

Pen and Paper Approaches and the Use of Artwork

Through all generations and across all cultures human beings have made marks on surfaces. Styles, techniques, colours and materials may vary but the purpose remains the same: self-expression and communication. There is something very immediate in the expression of oneself through artwork. Whether by pen, brushstroke, or other means, art involves the direct manipulation of materials. Transformation comes as the blank canvas receives colour and its flat surface appears to take on depth and form.

In the counselling room the directness of art can be an asset. When working with people who are nervous, or wary of being controlled (having words put in their mouths, for example), it can be valuable for the counsellor to blend into the background while the 'work' goes on in the contact between the client and the art materials. Directing someone towards felt-tips, paints or pastels, therefore, can be a non-intrusive intervention. However, there are times when the same intervention can feel threatening. Many people were humiliated during schooldays and now suffer 'performance anxiety' when required to take part in an activity which is redolent of school art classes.

I have a colleague who is both a therapist and an artist. Sometimes, in response to her suggestion that they use the various art materials available, clients retort 'I'm no artist' in a panicky or self-derogatory way. In reply, she tells them that this is a good thing as artists find it

difficult to use art materials therapeutically. I presume that she is referring to the fact that an artist is likely to be in the Adult ego-state; assessing form and colour, texture and composition. This may be necessary if
a work of art is the desired outcome, but is less helpful in the therapeutic environment. Here, it is more profitable for clients to be functioning in their Child ego-state; in touch with feelings and intuition.

When I invite people to use art materials I often preface that invitation with the assurance that it is not necessary to have any particular
skills in art in order to benefit therapeutically from techniques utilizing art materials. Sometimes we both know the next stage: if a person
has been talking about a particular dilemma or image then the usual
beginning is to represent that on the paper. On the other hand, people
may simply be feeling blocked or in touch with an emotion it is hard
for them to identify. Then, I am likely to suggest that they pick up a
felt-tip pen (or whatever other tool is available) and begin making
marks on the paper without censoring or processing the endeavour.
The unconscious takes over quite quickly and they soon find themselves in touch with the material they need to deal with: their most
pressing open Gestalt.

One woman was feeling sad but did not really know why. She began
by drawing some flowers in a rather traditional-looking way and I
assumed she was behaving as though in an art class. Next, she drew two
red intertwined hearts linked to the flowers. As she started talking
about what she had drawn, we both realized that her sadness was due to
unexpressed grief. An estranged brother had died and she had felt con-
strained by the rest of the family to behave as if he had never existed.
Equipping her unconscious with paper and a few pens had quickly
shown (by the two hearts) that she had loving feelings towards him, and
(by the flowers) that she needed to mark his death in some way.

Journals and Clients' Work between Sessions

Many of the people I see keep a journal: some begin it prior to starting counselling while others embark on it as a means of recording our
sessions and of continuing the work between sessions. In some cases a

percentage of journal entries are in a visual rather than a verbal form. Having worked with images in their journal, some clients bring what they have depicted to provide a focus for the next session.

For others, the process occurs in the opposite direction: if a particularly strong image or theme has emerged during a counselling session, I sometimes recommend that people use as many modalities as possible to familiarize themselves with it and fully 'own' it. As well as writing it up, I suggest that they draw or paint it (and perhaps even find a tactile means of representing it – perhaps through clay). Reinforcing an image in this way increases its integration into our self; and therefore fosters our own journey to wholeness.

Later, in chapter twelve, sections from a woman's journal are reproduced. There, Tace describes how she brought her artistic skills to bear to deepen the work we were doing to help her overcome a phobia. Tace was morbidly afraid of feathers and we had adopted a multimodal approach to therapy including behavioural and cognitive work. A major element of the latter was the reframing of feathers from being seen as something sinister, deadly and tremendously ugly, to being perceived as a part of that natural world which Tace loved and appreciated. Tace decided to reinforce this new attitude by including feathers in one or two pictures. In so doing she was carrying out a behavioural procedure, by being in close proximity to the thing she feared, while feeling comfortable and relaxed as she painted. Artwork for Tace, then, proved to be a valuable way to bring together useful aspects of the various approaches we had used.

At a workshop on supervision, Brigid Proctor introduced a deceptively simple, non-threatening exercise which my colleagues and I have since found consistently valuable. Brigid merely asked us to get into pairs and take turns at depicting ourselves and a particular supervisee as fish on the page. (Needless to say this basic concept can be extended to include, for example, a client depicting himself and his wife, or a counsellor depicting herself and her client.)

Brigid then made various suggestions as to how to work with the fish images. She recommended that both partners stay silent while the drawing is being executed, and remain silent as both look at the completed work. The partner can then hold the picture at arm's length for the artist to gain a different perspective. When the two do speak, she warned against the partner making interpretations ('You've used a lot of brown. You must be depressed'; 'This fish is very small. You've obviously got low self-esteem') but instead to make observations about process ('You seemed to press harder in this area. This part of the page has stayed blank'). Interpretation of a person's material is generally frowned upon, of course, in many forms of counselling. To have our words, actions, beliefs and motivations interpreted accurately (but prematurely), or to have them distorted by being interpreted inaccurately, is to suffer damage. Brigid also suggested that the person who had produced the picture feel his or her way into the identity of each fish and speak as each in turn.

At that workshop I was very impressed with the speed and accuracy with which unconscious and subconscious material was represented. I suspect that the instruction as to what to draw helps some people who may feel threatened by simply being invited to let the pens make marks, or to draw 'anything'; while the choice of a fish as the element to be created allows for anything from a single (Ichthus-like) stroke, to a fantastically detailed creation.

Art in a Group Setting

There are a great many ways to use art in both individual counselling and group work, ranging from the very simple to the more elaborate. Most approaches can be used in either setting, with a little adaptation.

A useful warm-up is for the facilitator to place on the floor lots of pictures (ensuring there are several more pictures than people). Pictures can be of any kind but typically are picture postcards, photographs from glossy magazines and reproductions of works of art. Group members are then invited to study the pictures for a while, before selecting one with which they identify. The group then splits into pairs, each with their chosen pictures.

In their pairs they take turns to describe their picture, and then themselves in exactly the same words and phrases. The insights gained can be profound and participants often find themselves in touch with deeply significant material. An extension of this, from co-counselling, is for the partner to repeat to the first person all the statements.

In one personal growth group, Maria selected a picture of an old rugged house. She began by saying, 'The house is old and battered but well-loved. It is beautiful and solid and its scars add to its beauty.' By the time she was half-way through repeating this as '*I* am old and battered...' she was in tears. Her partner, holding steady eye contact, then told her 'You are old. You are battered. You are well-loved...', continuing to repeat again any phrases which evoked particular emotion. Then it was Maria's turn once more, to make the same statements and notice an increasingly strong sense of being able to 'own' them. Maria wept a great deal through this, yet described the experience as freeing, exhilarating and healing.

A set of photographs, originally designed for sparking discussion in teenage groups, has also proved useful in adult groups. The scenes depicted are slightly quirky, such as a baby holding a telephone receiver; a set of signposts; two gravestones; a youngster at a harbour and a man and a policeman in conversation.[1] In a therapeutic setting they have been useful for putting people in touch with quite deep feelings. A man who chose the photograph of the baby and telephone was soon sobbing about his isolation in childhood, while a woman who chose the signposts rapidly progressed from superficial comments to a cry of despair – even dereliction – expressing her inability to know where to turn, or to sense God's direction in her life.

In my counselling room I have a large painting, executed by my artist colleague. I describe it in more detail in chapter thirteen, when presenting Keith who worked with it on a number of occasions. Basically it shows a large swirling mass; grey, becoming black; with a brilliant white oval above, surrounded by patches of rainbow colours.

Often a client has remarked directly on the picture, or made a comment which I feel leads naturally to working with it. At this point I move the canvas to a point where we can both see it easily and invite the person to focus on it. Or they may have made a statement like 'I feel as if I am falling into a dark hole' or 'Everything seems black' in which case I ask them to concentrate on the blackness in the picture.

Sometimes I use this picture as a warm-up in groups. I invite participants to gaze at the picture, and notice what they perceive. I emphasize the fact that there is no right or wrong perception. After a few minutes I may suggest that people either pair up and share their perceptions, or that each participant describes to the group what they have seen in the picture.

Each time I am struck by the variety of responses. Usually the dark area is regarded as more 'negative' ('heavy', 'frightening', 'oppressive', 'depressing') than the white and the rainbow. Words such as 'brilliance', 'heaven', 'space', 'promise', 'potential' and 'joy' tend to be ascribed to these. However, not everyone conforms to this pattern. Some regard the white area as threateningly empty, and the black as more cosy.

Then there are those (presumably many Myers Briggs S's) who are so unfamiliar with the language of symbolism that they can only respond in terms of colour, shape and approximate representation – 'I can see a thing like a hockey stick'; 'There's a sort of number six in there'. (Having someone in a group who genuinely responds in this way tends to flummox the other participants, while their ability to read all sorts of things into the picture tends to bemuse the one who does not do so.) In this case, it is vital that everyone's contribution is considered equally valid and that one person does not feel rejected or marginalized.

You may choose to persevere, and more or less teach such a person how to 'read' symbolism, by taking a step-by-step approach: 'You see that this part is black and this part is white. As you look at each, how do you *feel*? Are you aware of any reactions in your body? Do any memories, thoughts or images come to mind?' (If the answer to either of the latter two questions is 'yes', you can then help the person explore the associations between the marks on the canvas and the specifics of their response.) On the other hand, you may decide that an endeavour of this kind would be too time-consuming, and choose instead to focus on other ways of working. (Though if time is not a major consideration, the person's interests are probably best served by having their horizon broadened by being opened up to the language of symbolism.)

Pen and Paper Approaches

The therapeutic work one does with each person is, of course, unique – and so are the ways in which the various creative tools are utilized with each individual. This perhaps applies particularly to pen and paper techniques as the possible range is so wide, encompassing activities governed by both the left and right sides of the brain.

During an initial session I take a history – a largely left side of brain endeavour – using pen and paper. With many clients a pen never emerges again, apart from at the end of each session to be used to sign receipts! On the other hand, I may feel that a particular network of relationships a person is describing is complicated enough to warrant being represented on paper.

Genograms[2] have been developed as a way of representing information of this kind with particular symbols denoting divorce, abortion and so on. For visualizers they offer a simple, neat way to encode a considerable amount of material. Those for whom diagrams are relatively impenetrable without a good deal of effort would probably not assign them much value. Constructing a quick network allows me to understand the complexities of, say, a large extended family. (Once I have drawn a rough family tree I am more likely to remember whether it was Auntie Ethel or cousin Hilda who was killed, necessitating some family discontinuity or other – an example of reinforcing information by presenting it to multiple modalities.)

On other occasions, compiling a representation of their important networks brings insight for the client, even though I may initially have chosen this method in order to clarify a situation for *my* benefit. One supervisee, for example, feeling unsupported by her superiors, changed her perception after seeing the hierarchical diagram I constructed as she talked. When she appreciated the many levels within the line-management structure between herself and her most senior manager, she comprehended why, during a recent interview, he had seemed to have little knowledge of her job description. There followed the realization that it was actually her immediate superior by whom she felt let down.

When someone is grappling to describe a complex situation, I invite the person to represent it spatially, or I may choose to do so myself.

This helps both of us to grasp the connections between elements, or the range of options available. And I quite often use pen and paper as a teaching aid, depicting ego-states, for example.

Individual or Group Work

Sometimes I recommend 'homework' involving pen and paper. One simple exercise I quite often suggest for people whose self-esteem has been damaged, is that they write their first name in the middle of a large sheet of paper, then around it place as many positive attributes, achievements and skills as they can bring to mind. Some are then brave enough to attach it to their fridge, or in some other place open to scrutiny by friends and family. Most prefer to bring it to their next appointment, and spend that session owning more fully the qualities they had listed and, perhaps, identifying others.

This exercise lends itself to use in a group – as do other pen and paper approaches. One I have adapted in various ways for different groups involves inviting participants to imagine their life as a journey. On this 'road' I then ask them to depict major events – births, deaths, transitions and so on – or special relationships, such as those people (grandmother, Sunday School teacher, close friend, perhaps) who have offered unconditional love. The level of drawing skill required is minimal: simply a wavy line to represent their life's journey. Events and people can be entered as symbols (such as a black cloud to represent a bout of depression), or names and phrases can be used. In a group setting, members can be invited to produce their drawing on their own, then divide into pairs with each person talking in turn, without interruption, describing their journey and the people and events they have depicted. The next stage depends on the purpose of the group. If the group has gathered to learn listening skills, then teaching points about giving full attention without interruption can be made. Used as an ice-breaker for a new prayer and Bible study group, this exercise leads naturally onto prayers of intercession and thanksgiving. In a counselling group, seeing their lives depicted in this way can trigger a specific piece of therapeutic work such as mourning one of the 'special' people who has now died.

Many counselling courses teach approaches recommended by Gerard Egan.[3] One, used in other settings as well as therapy, is Force-field Analysis. In this technique, the counsellor and client identify the set of forces which are exerting pressure *towards* a specific desired change (facilitating forces) and those which militate *against* that change (restraining forces). Using pen and pencil (or blackboard and chalk or, in a group, an overhead projector) the two sets of forces are shown as arrows going upwards (towards change) or downwards (against change). Seeing an aspect of their life represented in this way focusses and clarifies people's thinking. They are enabled, as it were, to 'see the wood for the trees', after which tackling one or more of the restraining forces seems more feasible.

Many counselling courses include 'Johari's Window'[4] in a self-awareness module. A stylized window (a crosspiece set in a square) is drawn and people are invited to consider the different kinds of personal information contained in each quadrant. The first contains information which is freely available to anyone such as eye colour; the second contains information which the person knows, and may choose to share: such as a prejudice or fear; the third contains information which others have but the person does not: this includes such things as the specific effect their presence has on others; and the final square includes information which is hidden from both the person and everyone else: material in the unconscious of which no one is aware. Carried out in pairs this is designed as an exercise to improve participants' self-disclosure skills and to increase their self-awareness.

Some obvious advantages of using exercises in groups are the elements of sharing and of consensual validation, that is, checking one's own responses against those of other people. By these means people come to realize that they are not 'odd' or unusual but that other people have unexpected secrets, unpredictable reactions and other quirks, all enhancing their humanness. Also, a unanimous opinion sincerely expressed by members of a group on the subject of one's personal qualities often counts for a good deal more than the opinion of a single person – such as spouse, close friend or counsellor.

Using pen and paper techniques in a group setting, then, can be especially valuable.

Psychometric Testing

There is a long history of pen and paper tests in psychology – the so-called 'psychometric tests' which determine an individual's score or profile on some attribute or set of attributes. While many can only be administered by trained personnel, it is useful for counsellors to be aware of their existence.

Some counsellors make use of diagnostic tests to determine, for example, the depth of a person's depression. These are mainly left side of brain procedures, and therefore outside the scope of this book.

Counselling Keynotes

The range of possibilities is vast – from inviting a person to write a poem to handing someone a crayon to scribble with; from administering a published test to letting a person speak obliquely about a photograph. As with other techniques, I recommend that you only ask others to do things you have previously tried out for yourself, and only work in ways with which you feel comfortable.

Let people make their own associations and connections rather than imposing yours.

Gently help them own their projections – when they attribute characteristics to a picture, invite them to repeat the phrase using 'I'; or ask in what way they show the attribute they have mentioned.

Pen and paper techniques are useful as ice-breakers in group work. Consult some books of games (for example, the Gamesters' Handbook[5,6] *to glean some ideas. Use those described, then construct your own!*

1. *Write On – Rub Off Pictures*, Creata, Martock, Somerset (undated).

2. Monica McGoldrick and Randy Gerson, *Genograms in Family Assessment*, W. W. Norton, 1985.

3. Gerard Egan, *The Skilled Helper, A Problem-Management Approach to Helping* (fifth edn), Brooks/Cole Publishing, California, 1994.

4. J. Luft, 'Group Process: An Introduction to Group Dynamics' (1966), in William Stewart, *An A–Z of Counselling Theory and Practice*, Chapman and Hall, London, 1992.

5. Donna Brandes and Howard Phillips, *Gamesters' Handbook*, Hutchinson, 1978.

6. Donna Brandes, *Gamesters' Handbook Two*, Hutchinson, 1982.

7

PERCHANCE TO DREAM?

Dream Work

Dreams fascinate me. They possess an economy which is sometimes astounding, and can reveal huge amounts about a person's process: their characteristic way of being.

Dream interpretation has featured in personal growth activities and prediction of the future for thousands of years. Lots of books have been written about dreams and many people find the content of their dreams intriguing. Russ Parker has produced an excellent book, from a Christian viewpoint, which I heartily recommend if you are contemplating beginning to make use of dreams in counselling.[1]

I will begin this chapter with an overview of the subject to provide a backcloth against which I will then describe ways of working with one's own or other people's dreams.

Sleep and Dreaming

Research, carried out in sleep laboratories all over the world, has shown that all normal people dream during sleep. (Exceptions occur, for example, during drug-induced sleep and during short naps.) In the 1950s, Aserinsky and Kleitman made the startling discovery that two kinds of sleep alternate during the night.[2] At the onset of sleep a person shows little body movement; little brain activity can be measured by an EEG machine, and breathing and eye movements are slow and regular. This 'quiet' or Non-REM (NREM) sleep passes through several stages as the person gradually passes into a deep sleep from which progressively stronger stimuli are required to wake him. Then, about 80 minutes after the onset of sleep, the person's breathing becomes much faster and irregular; his brain temperature and rate of activity soar; his muscle tone decreases yet his penis becomes erect and his eyes move, in a co-ordinated manner, rapidly in various directions. This Rapid Eye Movement (REM) sleep recurs at approximately 90-minute intervals during sleep, and for progressively longer periods. The first episode of REM lasts about 10 minutes and by morning a REM period may last for up to an hour.

Different Kinds of Sleep – Different Kinds of Dreams

It is during REM sleep that most dreaming occurs, and recall is richest immediately after the end of the REM period; even five minutes after the end of REM sleep dream recall is fragmentary. Some dreams do occur in NREM sleep, but these dreams tend to be more like thinking than 'dreaming' as we usually understand the term. They are less vivid, less visual, more conceptual, more pleasant and more plausible. A third kind of dream should finally be mentioned. This is the hypnogogic dream which occurs at the onset of sleep and takes the form of strange bodily sensations, conversations or hallucinations, for example of disembodied faces. Hypnogogic dreams tend to be shorter, and no less dramatic than REM dreams.

The Psychology of Dreams

Most writers on dream content and interpretation give credence to the notion that a dream is a message *from* oneself *to* oneself. Indeed the words from the Jewish Talmud are often quoted in this context: 'An uninterpreted dream is like an unread letter'; while Jung writes: 'the problem of dream analysis stands and falls with the hypothesis of the unconscious; without this the dream is a senseless conglomerate of crumbled fragments from the current day.'

In its most highly evolved form this phenomenon of intra-personal communication can be seen in the creative results of 'Das Rheingold' (Wagner), *Dr Jekyll and Mr Hyde* (R. L. Stevenson), the foundation of nuclear physics (Nils Bohr) and of modern organic chemistry (Kekule) – each of which were presented, in more or less completed form, to their originators during sleep.[3]

Some people make further use of this intra-personal mode of communication by practising 'dream incubation', in which they focus on a particular problem before sleeping and request their 'intuition', 'Higher Self', 'higher unconscious', 'unconscious', 'Dream Power', or whatever, to provide an answer during sleep. This harnessing of one's own powers is practised by some mystics, and primitive peoples such as the Senoi people of Malaysia and the Iroquois American Indians, and is recommended by modern dream workers.[4,5] Russ Parker commends his readers both to pray *for* dreams to shed light on a situation and to pray *with* them to release and heal the feelings contained in them.[6]

Dreams and Religious Belief

For many ancient and primitive peoples, dreams are regarded as significant events that foretell the future, rehearse the past, provide evidence of bewitchment or communicate messages from gods or devils. In the Bible it is acknowledged that dreams can derive from activities which have occurred during the day (Ecclesiastes 5:3 warns that 'a dream comes when there are many cares'), but also that God can use this kind, or a more directly revelatory dream, to convey a message to the dreamer. In some cases the message was intended for the dreamer himself (for example, Genesis 28:12–15), while in other cases it was intended to be communicated to another person or to a whole group of people (for example, Matthew 27:19). In Hebrew thought there is a close association between prophesying and dreaming – a prophet is sometimes called a Seer – and it was acknowledged that God himself spoke to his people through dreams (for example, Numbers 12:6).

There are two kinds of revelatory dreams recorded in the Bible: those with an auditory message, which require no further interpretation (for example, Matthew 1:20) and those employing visual symbols, which need to be interpreted before the message can be understood (for example, Daniel 2). Numbers 12:6 supports this dichotomy: God says that He reveals Himself in visions to prophets and speaks to them in dreams.

Similar variations of divine message can be found in other traditions; for example, the dreams of kings are sometimes believed to have special significance for their subjects, while in the healing temples of Ancient Greece seekers of prophetic advice consulted priestesses who would dream on their behalf.

The Freudian Approach to Dreams

The work of Freud drew attention to dreams as clues to inner conflicts, and set the pattern for later approaches to dream analysis. His theory of dreams held an important position in his theory of psychology, and his writings are rich with detail and closely argued. Freud believed that the 'manifest' content of a dream could be unravelled in order to reveal the 'latent' content, and that 'the latent content of every dream represents the imaginary fulfilment of an ungratified wish'.[7] Freud believed that the latent content is distorted into manifest content for the purposes of censorship, so that the dreamer would not be shocked into wakefulness.

Freud describes five dream mechanisms or 'laws' by which the translation of latent content into manifest content is said to take place. These are condensation, displacement, dramatization, symbolization and secondary elaboration.

1 Condensation

This represents the over-determined nature of dreams, in that every element stands for several dream thoughts. For example, a room in a dream may have the characteristic of several rooms known to the dreamer, or a proper name may be a blend of two others. While all of the distorting mechanisms are means of evading censorship, condensation serves the additional purpose of expressing in the manifest content similarities between two or more elements in the latent content.

2 Displacement

In dreams, this takes the form of a transposition of significance between elements, such that the most striking features in the manifest content may actually be of little importance, while peripheral details may be of extreme significance. Reversals may also occur: for example, a dream may show the dreamer behaving towards another person in a way which the dreamer feels the other person behaves towards her.

3 Dramatization

This stems from the visual nature of almost all dreams. Just as a painter or playwright utilizes techniques to convey certain moods or the passing of time, so special expedients are utilized in dreams to indicate those things which cannot be directly portrayed. For example, the past and future may be unrolled before the dreamer, showing how an old wish that relates to the future may be realized in her present situation.

4 Symbolization

This refers to an equation in which one element is in the unconscious, and therefore to understand the symbolism the repressed equivalent must be found. To many lay people, Freudian symbolism is extremely sexual. However, as Freud said, 'sometimes a cigar is just a cigar'. Sharpe writes that psychoanalytic experience has shown that the ideas that are symbolized 'concern the fundamental basic factors of our actual existence, namely our own bodies, life, death and procreation'.[8] But, though the concepts and wishes which are symbolized may recur again and again, the dreamer's choice of symbols comes from material unique to him or her.

5 Secondary Elaboration

This differs from the other four mechanisms in that it arises from more conscious levels of the mind. That is, rather than coming directly from the dream thoughts, it stems from the more conscious mental processes and is an attempt to render the dream comprehensible.

These days, relatively few commentators take a strictly Freudian view of dreams, since experience has shown this to be too extreme and rigid. Faraday criticizes the Freudian view of dream mechanisms being adopted in order to avoid censorship and points out that a person may have a dream one night in which sex is symbolically represented, then have a dream the following night in which the sex act is frankly shown.[9] She and others also point to the tendency of the unconscious to depict images in extreme ways in order to bring the points to consciousness; indeed, Freud himself describes the dream mechanism of dramatization. However, in dramatizing an issue the unconscious sometimes produces images which are more bizarre, frightening or disgusting than the things they represent, so the notion of a censor must be called into question.

One example of this kind of dream occurred to a friend of mine. She had a terrifying dream of nuclear war which greatly disturbed her. However (in common with Hall's assertion that our dreams are personal letters rather than newspapers, and contain personal rather than communal material[10]), when she worked on the dream she found that the image of a nuclear war referred to an acquaintance with whom she was becoming more involved, but whom she had already recognized as being destructive. The dream seemed to be warning her against further involvement with this friend: a helpful, important message, but portrayed in such graphic terms that it is difficult to reconcile this with the notion of censorship. Of course, the Freudian view would be that the dream was not really about my friend's relationship with this 'destructive' person but contained infantile wish fulfilment. Nevertheless, it is hard to see how the image of nuclear war could be less shocking than whatever infantile wish she was supposed to be fulfilling.

The Jungian Approach to Dreams

Jung agreed wholeheartedly with Freud's emphasis on the importance of dreams as providing clues about the unconscious. However, he disagreed about dream interpretation, asserting that while dreams can shed light on infantile traumas, they always offer information about the *present* state of the psyche and indeed can sometimes point to the future. Jung disagreed with the notion of a censor, believing instead that the obscurity of dreams is due to our ignorance of their symbolic language rather than to a deliberate intention to conceal their meaning. Baynes, a follower of Jung, likened Freud's notion of the disguise function of dreams to the assumption of an English visitor to Paris that the Parisians were talking gibberish in order to make a fool of him.

Jung believed that dreams often have an important compensatory function in that they represent the efforts of our unconscious to get us to correct the narrowness of our conscious aims. For example, if a dreamer's conforming, well-loved father is depicted as a figure of fun, the message from the dream may be that she should become less dependent on her father.

Jung insisted that no interpretation should be accepted as accurate unless the dreamer agrees with its correctness. However sure the analyst may be about a dream interpretation it is worthless unless the dreamer gives both intellectual assent and also 'feels' the truth of it.[11] But it should be said that it can be very difficult to refrain from feeling that an interpretation is 'right' and that the client is using denial as a defence mechanism. For example, I saw one client whose father had recently died while undergoing open heart surgery. She was feeling guilty at encouraging him to have the operation, yet said she could see no possible parallels between this and her dream (after his death) that they had gone together to the theatre, where he was taken ill but she did nothing to help.

Jung's other methods of dream analysis were to ask the dreamer what the symbols meant for her, and for him (Jung) to find out as much as possible about the various images – for example, from myths, archaeological evidence, folklore, etc. He used this latter method mainly for those dreams which left the dreamer completely baffled but contained symbols arising from the collective unconscious, that is, archetypal symbols which are universal, part of the inherited endowment of the human psyche.

Jung believed that dreams reveal the presence in all of us of unexpected resources and unconscious wisdom: just as our physical bodies have a tendency to heal themselves, so we have a tendency towards psychological health. By presenting compensatory images or archetypes, our personal or collective unconscious can use dreams to show us the way towards health and maturity. For example, the 'shadow' (the alienated, rejected parts of our personality) may force itself on our attention by appearing in our dreams as a figure such as a beggar or gypsy.

Jung preferred to work with series of dreams, rather than single dreams, as one dream often throws light on another, and because it is possible to assess a person's movement towards psychological wholeness by examining changes in dream content. He believed that people could and indeed should perform their own personal dream work outside the consulting room and it was he who developed the notion of dreamers conducting dialogues with their dream images: a method later adopted by Perls.

The Gestalt Approach to Dreams

Perls dismissed the psychoanalytic method of using free association to trace a dream back to some infantile trauma or unfulfilled wish. He preferred to concentrate on helping people reclaim parts of their personality which they had rejected in order to avoid pain. He also rejected the notion of the unconscious and focussed on what insight a dreamer could obtain about herself in the 'here and now'. He called dreams the 'royal road to integration' and saw them as providing existential information, giving us messages about how we see ourselves in the world at the moment. Perls developed Jung's notion of every element in the dream being a part of the dreamer:

In attempting to interpret a dream, at the beginning, at least, regard all persons in it and all the features of it as projections – *that is, as parts of your own personality. After all, you are the maker of the dream, and whatever you put into it must be what is in you and therefore available for constructing the dream.*[12]

Using Perls' method the dreamer conducts dialogues between the images.

When they fight, the dreamer knows he has hit on something important. Whenever the mind goes blank or he feels sleepy, he knows he is trying to avoid something...the aim is to bring the fragmented parts of the personality into harmony with each other so that they help, not hinder, our growth. 'The best way to use a dream,' said Perls, 'is not to cut it to pieces and interpret but to bring it to life and relive it.'[13]

Some Gestalt therapists utilize a 'hot seat' so that the dreamer can change places while carrying out the dialogue. Using the 'I am...' approach described earlier, the dreamer first 'becomes' one of the dream images and then switches chairs and becomes another. The two may enter a dialogue, with the person moving between the two positions as appropriate. Other therapists prefer not to use this method for dreams as they encourage the dreamer to enter a different state of consciousness and this can be affected by the change of location and posture demanded by chair work.

Quite often the dialogue reveals the subpersonalities of 'topdog' and 'underdog' which Perls calls the two 'clowns' of the personality, constantly engaged in an energy-sapping conflict beneath our conscious awareness. Both the authoritarian topdog and the wheedling underdog strive for control. They may be represented in a dream, for example, as a policeman and an errant motorist: 'You can't go that way, you know. You're going the wrong way down a one-way street!' 'Sorry, I lost my way. I'm always making mistakes like that. You've got to make allowances for me.' These two 'clowns' can be integrated by means of a dialogue between their representative images in the dream; or, if working in a group, the presence of other people can be utilized and they can help the dreamer act out his or her dream. Alternatively, they can be receivers for underdog's messages: for example, the dreamer could go round the group saying 'I know where I'm going!' to each member in turn, in order to express underdog's newly found sense of competence.

If people have difficulty in acting out a particular image they are probably reluctant to reclaim that fragmented part of themselves. The more fragmented people are, the more nightmares they are likely to have, while people who are more self-aware tend to remember more dreams than other people. (Gestalt therapists are perhaps a little too dogmatic about this: for example, women have fewer REM periods and lower dream recall immediately before and during menstruation and they have more REM episodes and greater dream recall around ovulation. Therefore, suggestions that a woman is 'blocking' or not self-aware may be unfounded as her lower level of dream recall may be due to physiological fluctuation.) Also, dream recall is best immediately upon waking, so people who 'come to' slowly and remain groggy for several minutes are less likely to report having many dreams. On the other hand, jolting suddenly into wakefulness, for example, in response to a particularly strident alarm clock, tends to obliterate memory for a dream.

The Transactional Analysis Approach to Dreams

Rather little has been written about dreams from a Transactional Analysis point of view, although Eric Berne recommends that therapists ask about dreams at the first session with a client, as he regards them as presenting a picture of the client's life-script and world view. In addition, certain characters in dreams can be taken to represent the three ego-states (Parent, Adult, Child) while the dominant feeling present on waking is regarded as the 'racket' (defined as 'self-indulgence in feelings of guilt, inadequacy, hurt, fear and resentment'[14]). A man may report a recurring dream of trudging along a seemingly endless road from which he awakes with feelings of despondency bordering on despair. He would appear to have a life-script of the type known as 'going nowhere' and may often be swamped by feelings of hopelessness: his racket.

Many dreams can certainly be understood from a Transactional Analysis perspective. I recall one man who repeatedly dreamed of a policeman, a professor and a child: in this case the links to ego-states were easy to make. However, not all dream characters can be so simply categorized and, as different dreams leave one with different feelings, it is difficult to understand how the feelings present upon waking can always be one's racket feeling.

As with other aspects of therapy, I prefer to be flexible, using Freudian, Jungian, Gestalt, Transactional Analysis and spiritual approaches as seem appropriate, as I shall describe in the next section.

My Own Approach to Dreams: Personal Work

More than 12 years ago I wrote about the use I was then making of dreams in my personal growth work. I reproduce here what I wrote then.[15] A busy career and two children later, I no longer make any attempt to record as many dreams as possible. Nevertheless, there are mornings when I awake, knowing intuitively that I have had what is sometimes known as a 'big' (that is, significant) dream. On those occasions I still take the time to recall as many details as possible and to work with the dream in order to determine its meaning. The results continue to astonish and fascinate me, and I recommend that anyone involved in counselling should pay attention to their own and their clients' dreams.

> My initial step in working with my own dreams is first to **collect them** as thoroughly as possible. I keep a pad and pen, and a small torch by the bed (I have tried using a cassette recorder but only managed to collect two minutes of dream report and 28 minutes of quiet, slow breathing!). I remain as still as possible on waking and make notes as fully as I can, since recall is hampered by sudden movements and also deteriorates rapidly, so details not written down will probably be lost. I then slowly turn over, as it has

been found that dream recall is aided if one is lying in the same position as one was in when the dream images occurred.

Sometimes, while still in a semi-sleep state (and therefore, I believe, more receptive to the 'language' of dreams) I let my mind wander over the dream, **pondering** any parts which seem to be particularly puzzling or remarkable. Occasionally, I will use 'active imagination' there and then to **continue the dream** or I will **conduct silent dialogues** between elements in the dream, or **question objects or characters** about their significance. The next step, as soon as possible after the dream, is to **write it down**, in the present tense, as fully as possible.

I then attempt to **discern the quality** of the dream: is it giving me an obvious message which needs no further interpretation? (Usually this is blindingly obvious.) For example, a spiritual or pre-cognitive dream may contain just one message which is entirely logical, reasonable and sensible. In one dream, for instance, there was no visual content but a voice said 'Don't drink curdled milk.' The next day when someone was making me a cup of coffee I noticed that the milk was sour so I asked to have the coffee black. I believe that the intended meaning of the dream was to warn me about drinking something which could have had an adverse effect, although I do not doubt that, had I chosen to adopt another mode of interpretation and to '*be* the curdled milk' I could have used the dream in my personal growth!

In some cases the warning or message is slightly less obvious, but I follow Faraday in checking first whether, for example, a dream about my car brakes failing may be a warning from my intuitive part which has picked up signs of something being wrong with the car, before moving to **consider other interpretations** such as my inner 'drives' 'running away with me' or before I have a dialogue between the car and the brakes.

When a dream seems to need **interpretation**, that is, it does not contain any obvious message of a spiritual, intuitive or pre-cognitive kind, then I basically take a Jungian approach, applying the constructive technique of finding personal amplifications (for example, what personal significance do cars, or *my* car, have to me?), and exploring the mythical or Christian background. (This is less obvious in this dream, but may include references to biblical characters or mythological stories from which parallels can be drawn to my own situation.) I would examine the naive interpretation (for example, car = drive) and also, where possible, **explore dreams in a series** and deduce the meanings of images from their appearances in different dreams.

I begin by writing down events from the previous two or three days which may have triggered aspects of the dream: the '**day residue**'. This is usually of little value in terms of the message of the dream as any number of persons, experiencing a similar event, will produce different dreams in response to it – if indeed they incorporate it into their dream life at all. However, this ferreting out of triggers makes an interesting pastime and sometimes provides fascinating insights into how the sleeping mind weaves certain images together.

My next step is to take the main dream images in turn and find all my **personal associations** to them, and also **amplifications** (from reference books on myths, etc.). Sometimes aspects of one image may recur but disguised in such ways that only by **consulting works of reference** can I perceive the link between them. For example, I dreamt of a spider, and a fortnight later dreamt of someone I knew 10 years before called Lydia. About a week after the second dream I worked on the spider image in a Jungian way, having previously used the Gestalt method, and came up with the association of Arachne from the Greek myth. When I looked Arachne up in a reference book I discovered that she had come from a place called Lydia. Until then I had been rather stumped by the dream about Lydia, in that I could come up with few associations to her as a person once known to me, or as a biblical character (the only two associations I could think of). Seeing the clear link between Arachne and Lydia enabled me to treat these two dreams as being two from a series, and to find messages in each, and a sense of both continuity and movement.

Having found all the possible personal associations, amplifications and naive interpretations I can in a dream image (without,

I confess, making special trips to a reference library), the symbols may fit together in a way which is clear and gives a feeling of '**resonance**', that is, of the interpretation being 'right'. In this case I sometimes stop there but if the dream seemed particularly powerful, or if I do not yet experience the feeling of resonance I move into a **Gestalt mode** and set up dialogues between the characters, objects and images in the dream until a **conflict** is uncovered. I then continue the dialogue until some resolution is achieved. At times the Gestalt approach leads me into quite different areas, providing me with **different existential messages** from those I had come to by Jungian means. When this happens it seems to be either due to the Jungian search for amplifications having been 'barking up the wrong tree' (if I had not had a feeling of resonance); or confirmation of the over-determined nature of dreams; or a case of my unconscious having been given permission to 'work' and so setting about closing some figural Gestalts, even if the link with the dream images is somewhat tenuous.

Sometimes I use other methods in addition, such as exploring the **conceptual structure** revealed in my dream, or by **retelling the dream**, recognizing each element as a part of myself, for example, a dream in which a toddler is begging for food I might re-tell as 'my Child part is pleading for nurture'. If I feel dissatisfied with a dream's ending I will sometimes **invent a new ending**, for example, through active imagination or through dialogue visualizing a different outcome.

The most fascinating insight from working on dreams in different ways is that very often different approaches come back to the **same essential message**. One example of this is in the spider dream mentioned above. Immediately upon waking I knew intuitively that the dream's theme was motherhood and could easily identify a conversation from the evening before as the trigger. In dialogue I gained useful insights and a clear message. I did not know at that stage that spiders commonly represent motherhood, but when I later discovered this, using the Jungian method, I was able to make the connection between this dream and the one about Lydia in which motherhood had been the manifest theme.

The Senoi Indians, who advocate taking a conscious role in dreams, thus affecting the outcome, say that the dreamer should **demand a gift** from a threatening dream image and **request a gift** from a friendly one. Rossi writes that any dream image which is unusual, idiosyncratic, unique or odd is an **emerging part of the dreamer's personality**.[16] Rossi suggests one should **reflect** on it, to bring about new awareness; **integrate** this to lead to a new identity; **form** this to bring about new behaviour and **act** in this way to evoke new dream images. I have had few **lucid dreams**, so few opportunities to demand or request a gift. However, certain unusual or striking objects are often apparent in my dreams and I paint these, or make them in some three-dimensional form, record unusual words or phrases, and treasure these glimpses of different sides to myself!'

An Uninterpreted Dream — an Unread Letter?

A year after writing this I had a dream from which I derived enormous comfort. After 10 years of marriage and two miscarriages, I had just had my third pregnancy confirmed. My husband and I longed for children, yet were naturally very anxious as to the outcome of this pregnancy. Then I had a dream. I was travelling in a train when the ticket collector arrived. He looked at my ticket and said 'You've had two false starts haven't you? But don't worry, you'll get right to your destination this time.' Upon waking, I knew immediately that the 'journey' referred to pregnancy; the 'two false starts' were miscarriages and the 'destination' was a full-term healthy baby. I believed I had been given a crystal clear message that *this* pregnancy was going to be successful — as was indeed the case. I had (and have) no idea whether the message came direct from God or from my intuitive self, but my anxiety levels plummeted. Seeing my more relaxed outlook, my husband too, became less fearful about the outcome.

Often, we already have the answers to problems with which we are grappling, but they are stored in our subconscious and are therefore less easily accessible than conscious material. However this is the stuff dreams are made of, and dreams sometimes provide extremely clear answers to our questions. The pregnancy I have just referred to resulted in Thomas, our first child, who is now 11 years old and a keen inventor. He is currently planning a set of models based on 'Dr Who' characters. Last night, in bed, he was considering how to give the Daleks their characteristic voices. He woke up knowing how, because he had dreamed that he went into a model shop with my mother, and was talking to her about the problem. The shopkeeper overheard the conversation and said, 'This is what you need to do,' and rigged up the necessary equipment to show Thomas.

Sometimes it is clearer that it is indeed God who has provided a dream in order to convey a message. Sometimes, the dreamer 'puts two and two together' upon waking from her dream and contacts the person featured in it. At other times, a familiar authority figure appears with a succinct yet profoundly life-changing message for the dreamer.

On Sunday our vicar spoke of two dreams. On one night during the previous week he had awoken during the night with a parishioner's face before him. She was crying. He went back to sleep. Next day the same woman telephoned and asked to see him. Recalling his dream, he arranged an immediate meeting, and discovered that she had also been awoken the previous night by a dream. In hers, she had been about to go out when the vicar and his wife arrived. When she awoke she felt she could either take the opportunity to sort out a long-term problem or turn her back on it again. She decided to take notice of the message of the dream: hence her telephone call to the vicar.

One man told me about a dream he had had while seeking to find God through various New Age teachings and practices. At the time, he was working in Japan and in a dream his Japanese boss appeared and said (in English), 'You should read Augustine.'

When he awoke the man felt that he had been given an important message, although he had no idea who or what Augustine was. He wrote to ask his mother and she sent him a book of writings by St Augustine, which she had been given. This book helped the man gain clarity about God and was a very important stage in his pilgrimage, marking the end of his search down New Age avenues, and a renewed thirst for Christian truth.

This was neither a current nor recurring dream, and its message had been received, understood and acted upon, therefore there was no need for us to unpack it when he described it some years later. Nevertheless, the question of why it was the man's Japanese boss who not only conveyed the message, but did so in English, is fascinating.

One can only assume that the dream was telling the man to return to his religious roots rather than seek markedly different experiences or teaching. I would posit the following meanings for the various elements:

Japanese = different.
Boss = authority figure; the man's topdog, Parent part,
or spiritual self.
English language = the familiar in the midst of the unfamiliar.

Therefore, the executive function part of that man (topdog and/or spiritual self) demonstrates the familiar in the midst of the unfamiliar (those eternal truths that have been incorporated into New Age thinking) and points him back to his starting point (finding God through Christ).

Dreams in Therapy

During the initial session with new clients I ask about their dreams, particularly significant or recurring dreams in childhood or adulthood, and any they have had since deciding to come for counselling.

Recurring dreams in childhood may tell us a good deal about the person's concerns at that time. People who have been sexually abused, even if the memories are still repressed, sometimes report having had recurring dreams of being chased. Phallic objects may appear in these dreams: one woman, raped repeatedly by her father throughout early childhood, used to be terrified by a dream in which her father's wardrobe pursued her, his ties flapping through the crack in the door.

Recurring dreams in adulthood may demonstrate – incredibly succinctly – the person's real life process: a man who seems to be 'well buttoned up', reluctant to let his feelings show, may report dreams in which he makes repeated, desperate attempts to close doors and windows to prevent something escaping.

Dreams which occur around the time people decide to enter counselling are frequently predictive of the quality and effectiveness of the work we will do together. A dream such as 'I had been on a long journey. I didn't seem to know where I was going. I kept asking people the way but no one could tell me. Then I met this person who said she would show me the way. We went down a winding difficult path. Suddenly it opened out into a beautiful meadow', cheers the heart of a counsellor who can be certain that the client is ready and willing to work, and knows she has made the right choice of counsellor. On the other hand, if a person reports a dream at the initial session such as, 'I'm going round and round in circles. I seem happy enough, like a hamster in a wheel. Other people appear from time to time and say I should stop and I do try but then I go back to going round in circles', we may do well to seriously question the wisdom of agreeing to enter into a counselling relationship.

One of the aspects of dreams which I find so intriguing is the way in which they mirror the character, interests, and life style of the dreamer. I was counselling one man who was on long-term sick leave from his highly stressful job in sales. He was suffering from depression brought on by the demands of his job having finally taken their toll. He had had nearly 20 years of his working life ruled by his pager (an answering machine clipped to his belt) and I was struck by the aptness of the symbolism in his dream.

Neil dreamed he was moving from company to company seeing customers, always too busy to respond to the message that his pager was storing calls for him. When I invited him to 'be' the pager he delivered the string of questions stored on it:

'Where are you?'
'What are you doing?'
'When are you coming back to your family?'

When I later invited Neil to conduct a dialogue between himself and the pager, he repeatedly said he was 'busy', and would 'get to hear the pager eventually', while the pager made several statements:

'Do the important things.'
'Spend time with your family.'
'Prioritize.'
'Put off your customer. Respond to your messages first.'

Existentially, of course, Neil was living out the consequences of *not* having listened to his inner messages. Thankfully his marriage and family life had survived but his health had suffered a severe blow. He had already begun thinking that it would not be wise to return to his existing job: working with this dream confirmed and strengthened that belief.

Dreams and Supervision

I have had two recent dreams relating to clients, providing me with insight I needed on how to work with them.

The first example came after I had received a letter from a client and did not know what to make of it. I found one line (questioning my acceptance of her) hurtful, and did not know whether the statement was the result of the person's projection or transference, or whether it was tactless, deliberately hurtful or even whether there was any truth in it. The letter arrived two days before our next session. Pondering the various possibilities got me nowhere and I was aware of needing some clarification before seeing the woman, in order to respond in the most therapeutic way. That night before sleeping I prayed briefly for insight.

Next morning as I awoke I was aware of having had an important dream. At first the images meant nothing at all. Again a brief prayer – and then came the insight I needed. The dream featured a female vagrant and I knew instantly that this was an image of my client, who was feeling worthless and projecting this onto me. Sure enough she arrived for her session saying she felt 'rotten'. Quite clearly, her self-esteem had dropped very low, confirming my suspicion that her own lack of self-acceptance had been translated in her letter into a belief that she was unacceptable to others and to me.

(Events of this kind remind me how immersed we can get in our relationships with those we are helping, making it extremely difficult to see the wood for the trees. While still training as a counsellor I had a conversation with our then curate. He had just come from a difficult pastoral visit in which he had been called 'cold'. A conscientious, caring, Godly man, he was carrying out some painful self examination in order to verify this assertion. I recall the relief on his face when I said (knowing both people involved) that I was in little doubt that the word 'cold' referred far more accurately to the lady he had just visited and that, in my opinion, he could assume it to be a projection on her part. Nevertheless, here I was, about 13 years later, encountering a very similar situation yet being unable, at first, to recognize it for what it was. On this occasion the resources of prayer and self-supervision were sufficient but there are many occasions when we can only begin to see a situation with clarity when we take it to supervision. And our need for supervision – and the ethical requirement – continues for as long as we are counselling.)

The next dream was one I took to supervision.

I had been thinking about a woman whom I counsel, and wondering whether her slow progress justified her continuing commitment to counselling, or whether I should suggest either a referral to someone else, or a break from counselling altogether. The question remained unresolved and I dreamed about her that night. As I very rarely dream about clients I always take seriously any dream in which clients do feature. In the dream I spoke rashly to her, on the telephone, with the result that she hung up. I took this dream to supervision, saying that I wanted to understand its message. My supervisor asked me to re-experience the dream and tell it in the present tense.

After I had done so she asked how I was feeling on hearing the 'click' as the client hung up. In exploring my feelings I realized that I was experiencing regret at the sudden ending of contact, and the loss of all that was left unsaid. 'So what is the message of the dream?' asked my supervisor. 'Don't make a rash comment which would sever the relationship: there is still much that can be achieved,' I replied. This statement was accompanied by a sense of 'rightness' about my decision not to suggest that my client should stop coming for counselling.

Varieties of Dreams

Dreams, then, can be of various kinds. They may represent an attempt by our unconscious mind to unravel the complexities of a situation we are in; or may show, in symbolic form, a conflict between parts of ourselves. They may contain a message from our subconscious on a relatively mundane matter (a reminder of a friend's approaching birthday, for example); or provide warning of some danger or difficulty. They may be predictive, perhaps letting us know that an outcome will prove to be positive (or negative); or they may demonstrate our process by depicting a scenario with overtones (if not the actual content) which are deeply familiar to us. Finally, dreams can demonstrate healing we have received or (sometimes by occurring in a series) progress we have made in terms of our personal growth.

A single dream can function on several levels at once, with a number of themes interwoven, and characters and symbols playing several parts simultaneously. This demonstrates the creativity and inventiveness of our minds. On the other hand, one interpretation may 'feel' right and it may be a case of 'over-egging the pudding' to search for other possibilities.

Finally, a chapter on dreams would not be complete without reference to nightmares. Nightmares represent a desperate attempt by the unconscious to get the conscious mind to pay attention to something. In my experience, a single session of counselling has always put paid to nightmares, even those which have recurred for years.

When the person knows the 'cause' of the nightmares (for example, a bereavement, massive trauma or huge sense of shame about a particular event) I use general counselling techniques, and do not necessarily make any attempt to 'unpack' the nightmares. I usually finish with audible prayer if the person is a Christian.

When people do not know what message the nightmares are conveying, I invite them to re-experience the dream, and to tell it in the first person and in the present tense. As they do so the message usually becomes clear. While the conflict may well not immediately be fully resolved, it seems as though their unconscious breathes a sigh of relief at being listened to at last, and troubles them with no further nightmares, as they do the personal work necessary to bring resolution.

Counselling Keynotes

My first recommendation if you have not paid much attention to dreams in the past (your own or those of the people you counsel) is to read around the subject, perhaps beginning with Healing Dreams *by Russ Parker.[17]*

My second is to begin recording and exploring your own dreams in the way I have described. Pray for insight; take dreams to supervision; discuss yours with a trusted friend or colleague; study the language of dreams as revealed in biblical accounts. And, if at all possible, take some of your own dreams to a trained counsellor in order to get a sense of what this kind of work feels like.

Then, when you come to work with clients on their dreams, beware of disempowering them by taking a 'guru' stance. Let them stay in charge of their own dreams — just as they were the authors of them. Overall it is best to let all associations, projections and interpretations come from them. If you do venture to voice one, do so with diffidence, ready to reject it out of hand if the client experiences no resonance with it.

1. Russ Parker, *Healing Dreams*, SPCK, London, 1988.

2. E. Aserinsky and N. Kleitman, 'Regularly occurring periods of eye motility and concomitant phenomena during sleep' in *Science*, Vol. 118, 1953, p. 273.

3. Brian Inglis, 'Sweet Dreams', in *The Guardian*, 25 January 1984.

4. Ann Faraday, *Dream Power*, Berkley, 1972.

5. Patricia Garfield, *Creative Dreaming*, Ballantine, 1974.

6. Russ Parker, *op. cit.*

7. Ernest Jones, 'Freud's Theory of Dreams' (abridged), in S. G. M. Lee and A. R. Mayes, *Dreams and Dreaming*, Penguin, London, 1973.

8. E. F. Sharpe, *Dream Analysis*, Hogarth Press, 1937.

9. Ann Faraday, *op. cit.*

10. Calvin S. Hall, *The Meaning of Dreams*, McGraw Hill, 1953.

11. Carl G. Jung, *Memories, Dreams, Reflections*, Routledge & Kegan Paul, London, 1963.

12. F. S. Perls, R. F. Hefferline and P. Goodman, *Gestalt Therapy*, Souvenir Press, 1971. Emphasis my own.

13. Ann Faraday, *op. cit.*

14. Eric Berne, *Principles of Group Treatment*, Oxford University Press, Oxford, 1966.

15. Althea M. Pearson, 'Dreams and Dreaming: Psychology and Therapy', unpublished paper.

16. Ernest Rossi, *Dreams and the Growth of the Personality*, Pergamon Press, 1972.

17. Russ Parker, *op. cit.*

8

I AM A ROCK

Using Stones

Counselling evolved from various approaches which used verbal input as their main raw material. To a very great extent, concentrating on the verbal exchange remains the stock in trade of counsellors and therapists. While a Freudian may interpret the words, or a Rogerian may reflect them, focussing on listening to the words that are uttered results in such therapies being given the well-deserved umbrella title of 'the talking cure'. There are other possibilities, though, as this book demonstrates, and one way is to use tangible objects in the counselling room. Using actual things which clients can touch, move around and observe in relation to each other is a good way of helping people 'see the wood for the trees' when they are grappling with some issue or other.

Using Stones to Make Concepts Tangible

Some counsellors make use of all kinds of items, but one class of objects which many commonly use is rocks. In a basket in my counselling room, I keep a selection of stones which I have collected from the seashore. They vary in all kinds of ways: shape, size, colour and smoothness. Stones have many advantages: they are free; easily available; and familiar to everyone. More importantly, they are both neutral and yet carry considerable symbolism, as we will see. Their symbolism is especially accessible to Christians and represents both polarities, for example the stony, rebellious human heart, as well as the power of God evidenced in the empty tomb.

I often invite people to use the stones when I sense they are confused or perplexed about a situation. At other times, I use stones to help people make a decision which their rational mind has so far been unable to make. The first reaction of many people when I hand them the basket of stones is even more confusion, perplexity and indecision! I seek to reduce their 'performance anxiety' and assure them that there is no one 'right way' to use the stones. The complexity of the instructions I give depends on factors such as how long we have been working together: this affects the amount of trust the person has invested in me, and the extent of their familiarity with my working methods. Aspects of their personality may also help or hinder them in making the necessary conceptual leap and subsequent projections. My aim is usually to give as few instructions as possible, so that people have freedom to use the method as *they* see fit, rather than having my preconceived ideas imposed on them. I say something like: 'How could these stones represent the situation (your relationship, the people involved, or whatever)?'

I tend to keep what I say deliberately vague, unless doing so would raise a person's anxiety to an unacceptably high level. In that case I take a more didactic approach, perhaps giving some examples (while lifting one or more of the stones out of the basket to help the person over the barrier of actually making a start on this strange new activity). Most people are surprised at the immediacy of their response. They usually start without further ado to select stones to represent the various elements in the problem or situation.

Sarah, Arthritis and her Relationship With God

One young woman was feeling dissatisfied with her relationship with God. Sarah had been a Christian for all of her adult life and had received much succour from God. However, at that moment, He seemed very distant and she longed for renewed closeness.

It appeared that she had developed arthritis which was increasingly affecting her mobility. With three young daughters to care for, 'life is becoming more and more of a hassle,' she said. Many people had prayed for Sarah's arthritis, but with no appreciable improvement. She recognized that, without prayer, her condition may have deteriorated even more, and that often she had benefited in intangible ways from the times of prayer, but she nevertheless felt frustrated that God had not healed her.

Sarah was groping towards an answer to one of the most profound questions that human beings can ask. Some people had made platitudinous comments (which had frustrated her still further) about 'the will of God'. Others had taken a judgemental stance (which had left her feeling condemned) and urged Sarah to stop trying to fit God into the mould she had created for Him – to stop trying to 'call the tune'. And she had sometimes had her problems compounded in yet more damaging ways by people who let her know (in a manner which ranged from gentle through patronizing to frankly accusing) that the reason she had not been healed was due to unconfessed sin or lack of faith. Having no wish to perpetuate this process of traumatization, I decided to utilize a projective technique with Sarah, so that she could fully own the insights which came, instead of being left with the feeling that someone else's ideas or opinions had been imposed upon her.

I handed her a tray and placed the basket of stones next to her. With the minimum of words I asked her to arrange stones on the tray in such a way that they represented elements in her life and current predicament.

Not surprisingly, she chose the biggest stone (which also 'happened' to be pure white) to be God and put it on the tray.*

Next she placed a relatively large stone near it, announcing, 'That's me. The knobbly bits are my joints.'

She selected another stone, of roughly the same size, and placed it marginally nearer 'God' so that a little bit of 'Sarah' rested on it.

'That's Bob, my husband. He's a wonderful support,' she said. 'He is a solid person and very stable,' she added, indicating the underside of the stone which was flat, allowing it to rest on the tray completely firmly.

The children were next. Sarah chose carefully, selecting each stone because it somehow represented one of her daughters. A small white one she tucked partly under 'Sarah'. 'That's Becky, my toddler,' she said.

---

* Illustrations of stones based on originals by Thomas Pearson.

Then she took out a brown stone which had a black middle layer clearly visible.

'That's Susan. Her faith in God is a vital part of her make-up and shines out of her.' 'Susan' was placed nearest 'God' and touching all the other stones.

A mottled stone was selected for Amanda.

'She's a real mixture. Affectionate one minute but showing her fiery temper the next.' 'Amanda' was placed closest to 'Sarah' and 'Becky'. 'She loves helping Becky with things – she teaches her songs and helps her with things she finds hard.'

Sarah now had a configuration in which 'God' was separate from but close to a collection of five stones which were very near to each other or touching. She looked at them all for a moment, before selecting the final stone. This was of an irregular shape, with pieces jutting out. 'This is my arthritis,' Sarah said. 'Those bits are the claws or thorns it sticks into me.'

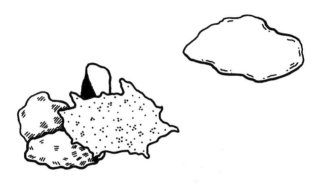

Sarah laid 'Arthritis' between 'God' and the stones representing herself and her family. It partly rested on those five. 'It blocks the whole family's view of God – our path to Him – not just mine.'

We had arrived at a vital moment. Sometimes known as an 'impasse', this can be one of the most fruitful moments in therapy. It comes when a person, having gone for counselling because of a difficult situation for which no solution has arisen, faces the sticking point head on. If the counsellor is steely enough not to jump in with solutions the clients themselves usually fight a way through.

Sarah had been bending towards the stones so I asked her to sit back slightly, to give her a wider perspective. She did so, and gazed for a few moments more. Then she looked up and summarized for me the insights she had just had.

'My real desire is to experience God's warmth and closeness again. I've been longing for Him to heal my arthritis [here she indicated the stone resting on the others] but He's not done so and may never do so. I've been letting my relationship with Him hinge on whether or not He heals me. *God* doesn't move so I can see now that *I've* got to: to come out from under the burden of the arthritis – to overcome it and come to God *despite* the arthritis.'

This insight had come from Sarah's own mind and spirit, prompted by the Holy Spirit and by my having provided an opportunity (some would say 'a space') in which the knowledge and understanding she already had could bubble up. She could now appreciate the truth of the words of those who had admonished her for setting her own agenda in her relationship with God. She could also see what had been pointed out in the manner of a wayside pulpit, that if God seems far away, it is *she*, not God, who has moved. The difference was that she could now own these truths, having come to them herself, rather than having had them thrust upon her.

From this new psychological and spiritual standpoint Sarah was now ready to institute changes in various directions: she had gained new resolve in getting her relationship with God onto a more satisfactory footing and she understood better what had been going wrong. This insight having been reached, another came to stand in the wings, ready to make its entrance: why was God not bringing about the healing she so wanted? Of course, this question had occurred to her many times before. Indeed, her frustration with God had been part of the 'package' she had originally presented. But the projective work had had the effect of sharpening her focus, of crystallizing the question, and of indicating that her true feelings on the matter are a good deal stronger than 'frustration'. Moreover, as a form of by-product of the method, she had acknowledged anew certain qualities in the people involved, and (literally) *seen* and *felt* truths about the family dynamic (such as her husband supporting her, and the different ways in which her children relate to each other) of which she had not been previously aware.

Ian and his Career Development

Are you familiar with the experience of considering a particular situation, and feeling a sense of unease which you cannot quite put your finger on? Or of regarding something in a negative light, without being able to identify the cause? It can be extremely useful in those circumstances to 'concretize' the components and thereby discover the things which are affecting you at an unconscious level. Any objects would fulfil the function of providing tangible representations of the elements but, having stones readily to hand, I made use of them when Ian was wrestling with the question of whether or not to apply for a particular job.

His personality is different from Sarah's, so he used the stones very differently. For Ian, each stone stood as an element in the question of whether he should apply for a job which he had seen advertised. He picked out stones, apparently without considering their physical features at all, and placed them in a line, labelling each as he set it down: 'Career development', 'Timing of a move', 'Work content', and so on. When all the elements were in place, I suggested that he experiment with the effects of removing one stone at a time. He immediately removed 'Work content', saying that he had no doubt that he was capable of doing the job. I then used reflective listening skills, as he spoke about the changing importance to him of challenge in his working life. For several years he had been in an extremely demanding job and had thrived on the challenges it brought. But at the moment he felt weary, longing to get off the treadmill for a while.

Next, I asked him to consider the stones and notice whether anything seemed to be missing. He replied that no spiritual element was represented – no mention of God's guidance, or of feeling 'led' into this proposed job. This realization led naturally to Ian telling me about another kind of job his boss had suggested might suit him. When he described *this* job, I noticed a change in his manner as he became far more enthusiastic and engaged with his subject matter. He spoke with greater confidence, instead of appearing almost to have to make an effort to talk. I reflected to him the differences I had noted in his demeanour and he confirmed that he had no real desire to apply for the first job we had been considering. 'My heart is with *this* one,' he said, 'so I've decided now not to apply for the other one.'

Ian, then, used the stones as (dare I say it?) a stepping stone into an exploration of issues surrounding the job they represented. Any stone could have stood for any of the elements. For Ian, any objects would have served the purpose as he used the chosen objects to stand for the various aspects of the proposed job in a holistic way, rather than taking account of the finer details and so using the symbols allegorically. It is important to allow people to use the stones (or other materials) in the ways that suit them and not to impose our expectations on them.

Christopher and his Feelings Towards his Father

Some people find that using the stones triggers reminiscences. Healing comes as they work with the memories which have been evoked. Christopher, for example, was pondering his relationship with his father. He slowly turned over a few stones, then suddenly selected one and drew it out of the basket. This stone resembled a toy car which his father had once carved for Christopher.

As he talked about the car, and the circumstances surrounding its creation, Christopher's positive feelings for his father were rekindled. He recalled their closeness and his father's willingness to join in with Christopher's activities. It was as though, as he talked, some of the dross which had accumulated in their relationship over the years was washed away. Simultaneously, Christopher saw his father again through adoring infant eyes – and appreciated him in a new way as he saw him through adult eyes.

Christopher's work with stones, then, involved him sitting, cradling a single stone as he talked about the memories which had been stirred by its resemblance to a precious object in his childhood. As he recalled the warm feelings from that time, he realized that they still existed: that his love for his father remained strong.

Sarah, Ian and Christopher used the stones in vastly different ways, yet each achieved their goals for that session: to work out how to restore a feeling of being close to God; to decide whether or not to apply for a particular job; and to clarify a relationship.

Diane: Using Stones for Stilling, and as a Vehicle for Intercession

There are as many ways to use materials such as stones as there are people, roles and situations. (In fact, there are more as these three interact to form yet more possibilities.)

A lay minister, in the midst of a medium-term counselling relationship with me, spent one session in a very different way from usual. Until then, our focus had been on her – her past, present and future. But on this occasion she arrived almost shell-shocked from the size and variety of demands which she had encountered the previous day in exercising her ministry. Diane believed whole-heartedly that God was 'big enough' to meet the immense and diverse needs of all those with whom she had been in contact – but just at that moment, she was feeling overwhelmed. Right then, she had a sense that 'the buck' had stopped with her; that *she*, somehow, had to meet their needs.

As I listened to Diane talking about her parishioners, with their problems of violence, terminal illness and financial strain, I felt that she would benefit from standing back from the details to see the whole picture – then offering the entire scenario back to God. We had not previously made use of the stones, so Diane had no preconceived notions of how to proceed. I just handed her a large tray and invited her to place stones on it, to represent the people she had been talking about.

The tray was soon dotted with stones. In the middle Diane placed a large stone which she said stood for God. Around it she placed others in various positions: standing on end ('she doesn't know if she's on her head or her heels'), and rolling ('that's me – always on the move'). She also used different shapes and sizes ('he has lots of facets; she seems so tiny'). Diane commented on the relative distance between certain of the stones and each other, and between the rest of the stones and the one representing God.

The pace of her speech had slowed by now and she was more reflective, more able to hear from God. I invited her to sit back and look at what she had created, and to think whether there were other people whom she would like to add. She selected stones to represent many of the people whom she had mentioned in the course of the previous few months' counselling. By now it was as though a symbolic representation of all her most important relationships was displayed on the tray. I asked her if there was anything she would like to change. With one movement she put both arms round the stones and edged them all in nearer the central, 'God' stone. 'I'd like the people to be closer to God,' she said. Placing an upright cross on the tray with the stones, I suggested she pray, taking each person in turn to the cross.

Diane spent several minutes doing so, remembering these people before God. I believe that her prayer now had a quality which it would have lacked, had she attempted to pray while still focussing so closely on the people's needs. Writers on prayer often urge the need to quieten ourselves in God's presence before we bring our petitions. They also sometimes remind us to look at God, rather than at the problem about which we are praying. This session achieved these twin aims and Diane herself felt greatly refreshed by it.

My emphasis, in this book, is on using and enhancing your creativity. Sometimes that means doing or saying something unexpected. Diane knew that our contract – our agreement as to what we do in our time together – is for counselling. Yet she was sufficiently keyed up by the encounters of the previous day to make me doubt whether we would be able to embark on any actual counselling. Instead, I chose to approach the same aims (of self-knowledge, resolution of certain issues and support) indirectly. The ensuing session could not, probably, be described as 'counselling', concentrating as it did on other people and on prayer. But I felt that the most appropriate use of our time together that day would be to temporarily change our contract. It seemed that my decision was vindicated: Diane's jittery feelings and difficulty in focussing on one thing at a time were relieved; she gained some insights into her tendency to take the world's problems onto her own shoulders and into her self-perception as having features in common with a blue, chipped marble; and she felt enabled to return to her working environment renewed. In the process, a considerable amount of deep intercessory prayer was offered on behalf of a large number of people. To echo T. S. Eliot, 'It was (you may say) satisfactory.'[1]

Using Stones in a Group Setting

1 Symbolism

If I am leading a day workshop I sometimes use stones. If so, I may ask participants to select two stones during the lunch-break and bring them to the afternoon session.

During the afternoon I invite them to take one stone in each hand and to concentrate first on one of them. I suggest that they ask the Lord to show them what it represents: what burden, hindrance or sin is weighing them down.

I then move slowly through the following stages, giving people time to focus inward and to glean the spiritual and psychological truths which come to the surface:

Let this stone represent some predicament or difficulty you are currently facing, or some aspect of yourself that creates problems.

Feel its weight; notice how it looks...Notice how you feel about it.

Now listen as God speaks to you about it...How does His attitude contrast with yours?

Now turn your attention to the other stone. Let this represent the stone that was rolled away from the mouth of Jesus' tomb. Feel its weight; notice how it looks...How do you feel about this stone?

Let God speak to you again...How does the existence of this stone affect your feelings about the first one?

Can God bring that same power to bear, and 'move' your stone – lighten your load in some way of His choosing?

You may wish to throw away, or bury, the stone representing your burden. But you may like to keep the stone representing the miracle of resurrection so you can hold it often and remember God's power.

I then provide participants with a handout (reproduced at the end of the chapter) and suggest that as they read it, they notice whether any of the symbolism from the other biblical passages is particularly relevant to them at the moment.

Finally I close with prayer, offering to God all the sins, burdens, potential and miracles that the group has silently considered.

Some participants want to say a little about the exercise, while others appear thoughtful, preferring to ponder the experience on their own before discussing it. I have used variations on this exercise in a number of settings and always find that people are amazed at what truths come out, and how God seems to speak to them. There are usually some interesting ideas generated, on the question of what should become of the stones. These range from throwing them into the sea to placing them on a prayer desk or at the foot of a cross.

Una Kroll, in *The Spiritual Exercise Book*, gives one meditation in which three stones are used.[2] She suggests that these represent 'a possession...which you could leave behind; a particular sin that weighs you down; an attitude, not sinful in itself, which may be hampering you from following Jesus'.

2 Projection

Recently, I used stones with mature students on a course in 'Counselling in Christian Contexts'. While they were considering the handout on stones in the Bible, I placed on the floor in front of them a selection of the stones which usually reside in a basket in my consulting room. I asked them to look at the stones and focus their attention on one of them. I indicated that they were free to choose any stone, and to allow the selection of that stone to well up from within – almost to let the stone choose *them*.

I invited them to pick up 'their' stone (a certain amount of turn-taking was inevitable at this point, as some stones were selected by more than one person) and familiarize themselves with it. I then said:

Notice how it feels in your hand...its warmth or coldness; its texture...How substantial does it feel?...What about its appearance?

Now jot down a few statements and descriptive words or phrases about this stone.

When everyone had completed this part of the exercise, I asked them to turn to a partner, and to list his or her stone's attributes to the other. Anticipating snorts of dismay or intakes of breath, I then asked the students to repeat their own list by reciting or reading it to their partner, but this time substituting 'I' for 'the stone'.

Having projection introduced in an experiential way such as this always brings some surprises. Outwardly compassionate people may hear themselves saying 'I'm hard and I've got rough edges. I hurt people who come up against me'; or shy people may find themselves saying 'I am beautiful, and very strong.'

While occasionally an individual cannot comprehend that any of the statements he or she made about the stone could possibly be personally applicable, by far the majority are willing to explore the possibility that these statements reveal attitudes about themselves. Helping people to 'own' their projections can be most rewarding, as they often sense an opening up of their internal world which is nearly as exhilarating for the therapist to facilitate as it is for them to experience. I recall working with a woman whose ability to make people laugh had been progressively deeply buried under her husband's very quick wit. It was as though she, who had been considered 'very funny' as a teenager, had handed the function of humour over to her husband, whom she perceived as being 'funnier'. Whether that was so was not for me to judge, and was not relevant. More to the point was that she had gradually constricted her ways of behaving and largely squeezed out her ability to bring humour to situations. It was a delight to watch her re-own this part of herself.

Since the exercise with stones demonstrates projection, and since we project those things about ourselves which are hard for us to own, it is hardly surprising that the exercise sometimes reveals attitudes and beliefs which cannot be immediately and joyously re-owned. In that case, part of the purpose of an exercise like this is to throw up the things in our unconscious which need attention. On the other hand, I do not advocate avoiding the use of projective techniques in a training situation or other group setting, on the off-chance that material will be thrown up for someone which is difficult for that person to deal with. Instead, I believe that gentle exercises such as the ones I have described here can be used in a positive way to facilitate personal growth. Should individuals feel threatened, the worst that is likely to happen in response to projective techniques used in this way, is that people will 'block' their awareness, and deny the truth of the statements when applied to themselves.

Postscript

After writing this chapter I came across a paper by Gordon Sleight who is a parish priest also involved in ministerial training.[3] He writes movingly of using stones with his own father when his father was dying in hospital. Drawing on his experience of using stones with theological students as well as with other people who were dying, he invited his father to choose one stone from a selection of palm-sized stones. He then asked his father to hold the stone in one hand, his other hand cupped over it, and to place into it everything (past, present and future) that was troubling him.

In time, he produced a bowl and invited his father to wash away everything he had put into the stone. Having dried the stone, his father again held it while he, his wife and Gordon placed their hands over it and put into it all the good things from the past and present, and hopes for the future. Finally, Gordon verbalized his love and that of his mother and of God, for the father.

At the end Gordon suggested that his father keep the stone to hold during difficult times. 'He looked me in the eye, thanked me and held onto my hand, the first real touch in more than 40 years, beyond formal handshakes in adulthood and the occasional clout round the ear in childhood!' Encouraged that the stones ritual had achieved the twin aims of helping his father unburden himself and proved to be a means of reconciliation between them, Gordon continues:

It opened up a very close and much more physically demonstrative relationship between my father and me in the last three weeks of his life. He was more relaxed, more open, more at ease with himself and with me. We repeated the ritual exercise with a wider family group a week or so later. He kept the stone constantly with him, often holding onto it even when he was asleep or unconscious.

One of the hallmarks of creativity is surely the ability to respond with flexibility, and in therapy this means being able to respond flexibly to a client's verbal (and non-verbal) messages. I had a marvellous opportunity to do just that today.

I am counselling a man who said that he regrets some of the things he has said to his wife during heated moments. 'It's as though I had a big jar of marbles, and I spilled them out onto the floor. Most are back in but some still aren't,' said Patrick. Rather in the manner of 'that's a cue for a song!' I immediately handed Patrick a small basket of glass nuggets (which closely resemble marbles) and I fished out from the tray of stones a few scuffed and chipped large marbles (between golf ball and tennis ball size), which I held out towards him in the palm of my hand. Although Patrick had not used the glass nuggets before, I sensed that he would respond positively to this, which in fact he did.

I suggested that he select individual marbles from those in my hand to represent those things which were lost when the 'jar' got 'spilled'. Talking about the great amount of love which the jar had held, he selected one marble, saying that it stood for love – the love that had spilled out and not yet been replaced. Another marble represented the forgiveness that was required before that love could be restored. He chose a third marble and declared that it stood for the guilt he still felt about the things he had said. Finally he selected a marble to represent the understanding which he felt was needed by both himself and his wife, in order to re-establish their loving relationship.

Patrick now had four marbles in his hand, and the session was fast coming to an end. Patrick is committed to doing a good deal of 'work' between sessions, such as continuing with a guided imaginative prayer which we had been using, meditating on a theme we had been considering and keeping a journal. I therefore decided to suggest that he take the marbles with him, until the next session, and I recommended a specific task which he might like to carry out, based on the work of Gordon Sleight.

I suggested that Patrick get a bowl of water and taking each marble in turn, put 'into' it all the negative feelings attached to it. For example, taking the 'love' marble, he could put 'into' it all the occasions on which he *and* his wife had not been loving towards one another. Having done that, he was to wash that marble to cleanse it from all the negative thoughts, associations and feelings before going onto the next. When all the marbles had had the negative feelings put 'into' them, and been cleansed, I suggested that he then take each in turn again and put 'into' them the positive associations attached to them. For example, in considering the 'forgiveness' marble, he could think of those times when he and his wife *had* shown forgiveness to one another, as well as imagining other possible expressions of forgiveness between them in the future.

Knowing that his marriage is basically sound and supportive, with strong lines of communication, I suggested that he could then find an opportunity to sit and talk to his wife, showing her the marbles and telling her about the positive feelings they now contained.

He was able to do so, and explained to his wife his desire to put back into the jar the marbles that had been spilled. This disclosure of his feelings of regret and desire for complete reconciliation strengthened the bond between them and they took steps to rekindle the levels of cherishing of one another which had previously existed.

Counselling Keynotes

The use of objects such as stones can put people rapidly in touch with unconscious material. Go slowly, allowing time for the processes of owning and assimilation of these disowned parts to begin.

Resist the temptation to place your own interpretations and projections onto the material. Insights should come from the person who is exploring the projections.

Remember the adage that we should only work with other people in ways which we have first experienced for ourselves. Experiment with stones on your own, exploring some problem or decision. As you do so, notice what questions prove particularly fruitful: ask yourself how you feel, what you sense and what you notice — about the appearance, feel and positioning of the stones; what is missing? what needs to be changed? and other questions as they occur to you.

When using stones, be aware of the large amount of symbolism which exists in connection with them and be ready to straddle the two worlds of internal, personal associations and cultural, spiritual ones.

Allow different people to use the stones as they see fit: sometimes this may be in very different ways from how you would have used them. Some will make selections based on the physical properties of individual stones. Others will pay no attention to their physical attributes, but proceed rather like a person in a café describing a scene to a companion and pressing into service the sugar bowl, cruet and whatever else comes to hand to play the various parts.

Finally, be prepared to use the stones creatively. Working with them requires right side of brain processes to come to the fore, so let the appropriate interventions bubble up as you take pains to stay with the moment-by-moment experience of the person you are counselling.

Stones Meditation

Mark 16:1–4

Jesus' body had been laid in the tomb and even while the women were wondering who would roll the stone away, it had already been removed. Can I trust the God who rolled away the stone from Jesus' tomb to remove the stumbling block in my life?

1 Samuel 17:45–49

In the story of David and Goliath, David killed *his* giant with a single stone because the battle was not his but the Lord's. The situation had looked hopeless, even ridiculous. What is the Goliath in my life that the Lord wants to slay?

Matthew 7:9–11
Jesus asks what parents, if their son asked for bread, would give him a stone? The Lord wants to do good things in my life. Can I trust Him not to give me a stone when I ask for bread?

Ezekiel 11:19–20
Ezekiel brings a prophetic word from God that He will give His people a new spirit and give them a heart of flesh instead of a heart of stone. When I feel hard, surly or resentful, I can ask God to soften my heart and give me again a heart of flesh, in place of the heart of stone.

John 8:4–11
John tells the story of the woman taken in adultery. Just as no one was willing to be the first to declare himself free of sin, and throw a stone at the woman, so I can acknowledge the sinfulness of all mankind and also the forgiveness of God. Jesus, who was sinless, forgave the woman, rather than condemning her.

Psalm 118:22–4
The stone the builders rejected has become the head of the corner – the large stone which anchored and aligned the corner of a wall. Do I relegate Jesus to the rubbish heap or do I allow Him to anchor and align the walls of my life?

1 Peter 2:4–5
Jesus is called the living Stone, the one whom the builders rejected yet the chosen one. And I, too, am called a living stone, built into a spiritual house.

Revelation 2:17
The Spirit promises, to 'him who overcomes', some hidden manna and a white stone with a new name on it, known only to him who receives it. This will be my eventual reward. But for now I can have a foretaste as I carry the stone with me and meditate on its rich symbolism.

1. T. S. Eliot, 'Journey of the Magi', in *The Complete Poems and Plays of T. S. Eliot*, Faber & Faber, London, 1969.

2. Una Kroll, *The Spiritual Exercise Book*, Firethorn Press, 1985, p. 19.

3. Gordon Sleight, *Contact*, Vol. 116, 1995, pp. 31–3.

9

'MOULD ME, FILL ME'

Using Clay

The Importance of Rhythmic Touch

Clay. Playdough. Plasticine. Dough. In some form or another most of us have experience of kneading a pliable material into a variety of shapes. We may have used modelling materials when we were children, and bread dough as we grew older, and so continued the activity into adulthood. Recency of familiarity is not important; repetitive manipulation of an object is genetically 'wired into' us and is a skill which develops early in childhood. Touching, caressing, palming: a young baby starts to show these behaviours at a young age, and soon finds them soothing and comforting. In addition, babies trigger rhythmic, repetitive behaviour in other people, who may stroke, rock or pat them; another reason why babies associate such movements with comfort.

An action such as playing with his toes, then, which is a naturally occurring behaviour, is rewarding when a baby does it himself. In addition, by the simple expedient of merely being a baby, he triggers further pleasant experiences by evoking caring behaviours, including tactile ones, in others. This, of course, represents the ideal. In dysfunctional families, or in some institutions, an infant's 'babyness', far from providing protection by triggering nurturing behaviour, instead creates threat and his vulnerability is exploited.

Human beings need to receive an ongoing 'ration' of a certain amount of physical touch. If babies are deprived of this, they may well develop a great need for physical comfort, which has been termed 'touch hunger'. Whatever a person's experiences in infancy, many go on to develop 'comfort gestures' – a remnant of the stroking they once did or had done to them. So, for example, a child who has had her hair repeatedly stroked as she falls asleep at night may hold her own hair at bedtime when an adult; or an infant who has a much-treasured 'cuddly' which he holds to his face may place his finger along his upper lip at moments of anxiety in adulthood.

We all know the healing effect of a hand on our arm or round our shoulders when we feel sad or worried. The calming effect is due to a number of factors. It communicates empathy, a sense that the other person cares and is 'in it with us'; it can also communicate the love of Jesus by being experienced as His arms in the situation. But that touch also functions at a different level, taking our unconscious mind back into those soothing experiences of touch we enjoyed in infancy, or providing partial compensation for the touch we did *not* receive then. In this connection, we need to be aware of retroflexive behaviour, which occurs when we do to ourselves what we would like to have done to us. When feeling sad, say, a mother may hug her child as a (very good) substitute for being hugged.

I was recently moved to hear that there are dogs living in some hospices, which have been specially trained to sit for long periods at the bedside of dying patients, with their heads within easy reach of the person's hand. The dogs have their heads stroked – on and on through the person's dying hours.

Pets are also used to ease the suffering of children who have chronic or terminal illnesses. An experiment in 'animal therapy' at the Hospital for Sick Children at Great Ormond Street has apparently demonstrated great benefits to the children of having contact with pets, both large and small. One child, who is reported to have become selective about which adults she wanted around her as she approached death, continued to gain comfort from the rabbits to which she had grown attached. Of course, dogs in hospices and rabbits in hospitals represent considerably more than just something to be stroked. Nevertheless, I feel certain that physical touch plays a large part in the gains reported.

In thinking mode, when we are applying logical thought processes to situations, we are engaged in mainly left side of the brain activity and exhibit mainly beta waves, which are faster. Just before sleep, or when we are engaged in right side of the brain activity, such as creative pursuits or a relaxation exercise, we show more alpha rhythms, which are slower. Similar brain waves occur when we are engaged in an activity involving rhythmic touch. Touch, then, especially when it is coupled with movement, has the effect of evoking slower brain waves.

Why Use Clay in the Counselling Room?

Perhaps it is becoming clear that inviting people to do some kneading in a counselling session can be potentially powerful. Almost immediately their speech and breathing usually slows and deepens and they begin to get in touch with material which, though always accessible, had not frequently been retrieved.

Kneading tends both to slow people down and quicken them up. Let me clarify that a little. When people are 'in their heads', or engaged in talking *about* their feelings or a situation, it is possible for them to be talking much yet saying little. Almost certainly they will be saying little that is unfamiliar to them. Presumably they have sought counselling because their own thinking has got into a rut, and that rut has not provided a way out. They may have heard themselves express the same thoughts over and over again, either in the form of internal ruminations, or in fruitless conversations.

Clearly, what they need in counselling is something different. In particular, they need to find a way to follow a different track from usual. Specifically, it is often of most use to direct them *away* from those familiar activities for which they use the left side of their brains – and *towards* activities controlled by the right side of their brains. If you take a moment now, and can conjure up a restful, lulling sense as you imagine using playdough, then you are probably switching into right side of brain functioning. At a physiological level, the predominant pattern of your brain waves will have changed to a slower rate.

The effect of this slowing on someone working with dough or clay is that the rush of verbal material reduces. As this happens, they begin 'working' – a term used in counselling circles to denote that a person is actually engaged in rearranging their internal world, rather than simply presenting it unchanged to the listener. By now, they are listening to themselves and having new insights about their true feelings.

And this is where the twist comes: now that they are working at a deeper level than before, and no longer simply proceeding down well-trodden paths, a wealth of new material begins to present itself which accounts for my assertion that the use of methods such as modelling clay both slows people down and quickens them up! The increase in insights, though, does not mean that people return to speaking at a fairly frenetic verbal pace. Instead, the 're-ordering of the interior' (to borrow an ecclesiastical term!) takes place at a non-verbal level. At this point they may stop speaking altogether for a while, or make only disjointed comments. If this happens, it is important to allow sufficient psychological space in which they can achieve what they need to. Profound discoveries can be made, far-reaching re-decisions made – *if* the person is permitted to do their work in their own way and at their own pace.

Clay or Playdough?

The choice of medium is yours. A Repetitive Strain Injury to my wrist renders it awkward and uncomfortable for me to use clay. Preferring to buy something which I, too, can make use of when I wish, I keep a tub of children's playdough available for use in my consulting room. My bucket of 'Soft Stuff' from the Early Learning Centre contains 'twelve rolls of soft re-usable modelling dough in 7 colours'. (Which gives it, to my mind, another important advantage over clay, which comes in such drab colours!) Some therapists favour plasticine which is easily available and comes in a range of colours but is rather harder to manipulate.

Of course, there is nothing stopping you from purchasing *both* clay and some children's modelling material. Clay has fewer 'childish' connotations, so may give rise to less resistance in a person who would otherwise feel it to be somehow undignified or even demeaning to be expected to 'play' during counselling. Clay also has the advantage of being directly referred to in scripture (though it perhaps takes only a small leap of the imagination to regard passages such as the story of the potter – Jeremiah 18, 19 – as potentially applicable to playdough and other varieties of modelling materials!).

When Might it be Appropriate to Offer Clay in Counselling?

As we have seen, using clay helps people move from left side of brain activity to right side of brain activity – or, to put it another way, from their head to their heart. Therefore it is possible to use this as a determining factor as to when to introduce clay. So, if I am seeing someone who seems 'stuck' in an unhelpful pattern of talking *about* things, situations and events, but does not seem to be actually 'working' with the issues which are being thrown up, I may well suggest that they may like to experiment with doing something completely different in one session. Usually, they are intrigued, but hesitate when it dawns on them that I am referring to their using *clay*.

The left side of the brain is associated with Adult behaviour, so it is hardly surprising that someone firmly entrenched in a left brain approach may feel threatened by the great leap into Child which they perceive as being required in order to use clay 'successfully'. Of course, there is no such thing as 'success' or 'failure' in this work. Yet, some literally recoil, their head rearing backwards, overcome by 'performance anxiety' and convinced they would have to be 'good at this sort of thing' for it to be of any use. They fear being seen as making fools of themselves. One man put it very succinctly when he said 'I'm not literate in this': a phrase which sums up beautifully his own emphasis on left side of brain activities which rely so heavily on competence in verbal endeavours; and therefore expresses his performance anxiety.

Another appropriate time to offer clay is when a multi-modal approach seems desirable. (This resembles the teaching method whereby teachers help children learn the letters of the alphabet by hearing, drawing and colouring them; and sometimes by feeling their shapes cut out of sandpaper.) If, for example, a person is exploring a particular theme in depth, then aspects of the theme can be reinforced by the use of various modalities. That is, after talking about and perhaps writing about it, the person may wish to paint or make a model of part of the theme. A related occurrence is when a specific image has emerged particularly strongly, say in a dream, or has recurred several times in different counselling sessions. A very useful part of the process whereby the person comes to 'own' the image, can be for him or her to actually create a 3-D representation of the image. In this way, people can come to face aspects of themselves, or of their past, present or likely future situation, from which they had previously been distancing themselves. Not only do they get to actually *see* the thing but can also touch, feel, create, modify, recreate and perhaps destroy it.

Here, of course, the importance of the sense of touch becomes very obvious. People may sit silently stroking an image or representation they have made. Soon, tears may trickle down their cheeks. At this point, they may begin to talk, or may continue working with the clay, perhaps altering or even pummelling the model.

It seems as though externalizing the issue, by creating an object which can be handled and modified, is sometimes a crucial step in a person's healing. Recall the references at the beginning of this chapter to the tasks of infancy. Babies learn chiefly by initially mouthing, and later manipulating objects in their environment. As we develop we learn to 'manipulate' abstract ideas by the use of thought processes – yet it remains true that we tend to learn more thoroughly when the process includes tangible, 'hands-on' experience. I am reminded of the Chinese proverb:

When I hear I forget
When I see I remember
When I do I understand.

The manipulation of ideas and feelings which are discussed here is perhaps governed by similar laws.

Using Clay to Bring Unconscious Material to the Surface

Rhythmic touch, as we have seen, brings profound changes to our current brain functioning (and may produce other physiological changes, such as a reduction in blood pressure). This shift into alpha rhythms is often attended by the emerging into consciousness of subconscious or unconscious material. Alpha rhythms can be encouraged by other means (such as meditation), but their effect when brought about by kneading can be enhanced by the 'rubber band effect' whereby touch evokes memories and feelings from a time in infancy when we received regular stroking. So a person may caress the clay, lovingly and meditatively, as they nurture their inner selves, providing the care for their adult selves which their parents provided in childhood. On the other hand, an action which appears similar may in fact be a retroflexive gesture, as the person does to the clay what he or she does not (and perhaps did not) receive from others.

Some people pound away at the clay, expressing their anger or aggression safely and satisfyingly. This may be accompanied by words, shouts or grunts. Others knead, apparently without paying attention, while talking. But their voice slows and deepens in pitch and when, after what may be a period of many minutes, they look down at the clay in their hands, they realize with a jolt that they have made a clearly recognizable object. It is fascinating to see how that object (like a dream) functions on many levels at once.

I witnessed an instance of this recently. Leah had experienced severe emotional and physical abuse in childhood. After some very draining sessions she said she would prefer that day's counselling to focus on current issues rather than resolving the past. She had not previously used clay, and I wondered how she would react. She worked the clay with her hands while talking about her strained relationships with her teenage sons, and her regrets at disciplining them harshly when they were young. Towards the end of the session she stopped talking, and her hands became still. I asked her what she had made and, seeing it for the first time, she said: 'A hand.' My thoughts went immediately to encouraging words from scripture about our names being engraved on

God's hand and God keeping us in the hollow of his hand. I did not offer these but instead asked her what associations *she* had made to the hand. She referred to punishment. Leah's clay hand, then, represented simultaneously her harsh parents, her own harsh parenting of her sons and God's perceived harsh judgement. The end of the session was looming, so I suggested to Leah that she might use a concordance to find references to 'hand' which she found positive and could meditate on.

At our next session, Leah handed me the clay, now just a relatively flat, formless shape. She said that when she had taken it from the bag to use, a piece had broken off. She had seen this as symbolic of the power of tyranny in her life having been broken.

The work with the clay set the scene for several sessions' worth of work. Some time later, she was given a small card on which was a photograph of a woodcarving of a child, cradled in a hand. I was delighted to find that she associated this immediately with her being held by God. I offered her the clay again and she created her own version of the image.

Leah gazed at the tiny figure, nestled in the protective hand and one or two tears coursed down her cheeks. 'He doesn't only wield a big stick, does he?' she said, more as a statement than a question.

Concretizing an Image from a Dream

Leah's 'hand' had emerged as an important motif as she had talked and kneaded simultaneously. For Pam, by contrast, an image to use had become clear between sessions. We had been working together for a few weeks, with a contract of exploring, reconciling and modifying her attitudes towards her parents. They had over-protected her, with the result that she regarded herself as immature and spiritually stunted.

Now she was ready to move on, to separate from them psychologically – but this seemed a scary new decision to have reached, and she was experiencing 'cold feet'. Then she arrived for our next session, feeling disturbed by a dream she had had the previous night.

Describing the dream to me took only moments as it contained no narrative but simply a single image. Pam had dreamed of a human head, its top flattened. I invited her to speak as though she were the head ('I am the head and...'); during which she soon realized that the head represented her, and symbolized her stunted emotional and spiritual development. 'I'm not rounded, I've got no form. I can't think and, what's more, I can't wear the helmet of salvation!' she burst out.

When someone makes a profound paradigm shift, or comes to a watershed, it is important to help them 'own' it as fully as possible. A multi-modal process reinforces the learning and facilitates its consolidation. It seemed important that Pam should form as close an identification with the head as possible, in order to fully own the fact that this was the way in which her unconscious self perceived her. Sometimes, we need exposure of this kind to bypass our denial and preference for the status quo and to provide the impetus for the change for which, at a deeper level, we long.

Therefore, I asked Pam if she would like to create an actual model of the image in her dream. She readily agreed and set to work. She first formed the head, with its flattened top, then sat for several minutes, stroking the top of the model. After a while she began, slowly and lovingly, to reform the top of the model, and to give it a normal shape. As she worked, I read the passage from Jeremiah 18 in which God speaks to the prophet about his ability to make and remake us as he chooses. As she continued stroking the model into its new shape, I invited her to sense God recreating *her*, to hear Him speaking loving words and caressing her with love, and giving her permission to grow into womanhood.

Pam then prayed a prayer of re-dedication and love. As she did so, she felt the Holy Spirit bathe her thoroughly from head to toe, which we both interpreted as God indeed remaking her.

Pam regarded this session as a turning point in our work together. After this, she gained the necessary resolve and resources to effect the healthy separation from her parents which she had long seen as desirable, but which had seemed unattainable until then. Her relationship with her parents remained friendly and loving, but as she said, 'I don't tell them everything now. I realize that I don't have to. I'm 25 and an adult and part of growing up involves growing slightly away from Mum and Dad. It doesn't mean I love them any less, just that I no longer live in their pocket.'

Using Clay in a Group Setting

Modelling clay can be usefully employed during the warm-up stage of a group session. Participants can choose a lump of clay (or playdough, plasticine, etc.) and spend a few minutes quietly working with it.

As an introduction to an exercise of this kind, the facilitator can invite participants simply to let their subconscious mind direct their hands, so that a figure is created without conscious thought or direction. Or the facilitator may prefer to suggest a theme or concept (fear, protection, the Love of God, for example) and invite group members to produce a figure relating to it.

In one group session I suggested that participants sit meditatively while I read the passage from Jeremiah 18:1–6 about the prophet at the potter's house. Then I invited them to create something related to those verses, or arising from their reaction to them. Some produced a figure they described as a 'blob' or 'shapeless mass'; others made something they said was 'many-layered' or which was 'long, thin: strung out'. One person described her figure as 'a star' while another said that 'bits are attached haphazardly'.

It is probably clear that these descriptions represent projections. I therefore asked individuals whether they could relate to feeling like a 'blob' or a 'star'; or asked whether they could connect with their life being 'multi-layered' or having 'bits attached haphazardly'.

In doing an exercise of this kind there are various ways to proceed. For example, it may be appropriate to invite people to bring their clay figures or 'pots' to a wooden cross and prayerfully leave them there. Or this use of clay can be regarded as a springboard into some other therapeutic method such as dramatic techniques or Gestalt.

In the case of Gestalt, the clay can be invited to speak ('I am the pot and...'). In particular, the figure may wish to engage its Maker in dialogue ('Why did you make me like this?') which can bring to the surface such feelings as anger, frustration or powerlessness.

Counselling Keynotes

For many people the rhythmic touch involved in kneading a pliable material such as clay or playdough contacts a deep psychological need for stroking and rocking.

Working with clay usually brings about a change in brain-wave patterns, evoking a slowing of speech and respiration, and a surfacing of unconscious material. Unresolved conflicts, memories, hopes, fears – people are often put in touch with deeply significant issues.

Allow time and opportunity for people to use the clay in whatever way suits them. They may concentrate solely on the clay and work in silence, or their hands may knead the clay, apparently independently of their thoughts and speech – until, that is, they suddenly recognize the figure they have created, and its place in their internal scheme of things.

For Christians, clay is especially symbolic. But don't be tempted to offer interpretations. Allow them to make their own.

Used in a group setting, clay can provide a trigger for personal work of various kinds. Be prepared to 'go with the flow' of what is happening in the present moment, rather than attempting to plan how the session will progress.

10

LITTLE RED RIDING HOOD,
OR GRANDMOTHER?

Using Miniature Figures

The human form is the most familiar 'object' in our world. We inhabit an inner world whose boundary is formed by skin and we experience human bodies – our own and other people's – with all our senses, at every moment and throughout our lives. In earliest babyhood many of our most crucial tasks directly concern the human form and its functioning. For example, we begin to determine where our bodies end and where the bodies of other people begin; we embark on the process of getting our own bodies to do the things we want them to do; and we start processing information about other people, based on the evidence we glean from their bodies.

Human babies are programmed to take more notice of a human face, or something resembling one, than of dissimilar objects. This reinforces the special value which is assigned to our bodies as uniquely important in creation. (Incidentally, it can be an eerie experience to feel that this uniqueness of the human body is being denied. This can occur when one has one's own body parts, such as hands, treated as inanimate tools or as an extension of themselves by autistic children, whose perception and understanding of people and the world is so different from that of most of us.)

The importance of the human body as a vital concept for human beings therefore seems self-evident. Moreover, ancient artifacts appear to suggest that human beings have always been mindful of human form. Mankind has created representations of the human body – whether as cave paintings or as crude dolls – for as long as people have inhabited the earth. Moreover, a great deal of the content of counselling sessions concerns people – whether clients' so-called 'significant others' or aspects of their own personality.

Human Figures

Human figures, then, in the form of dolls or puppets, seem an obvious choice of equipment for the therapy room. Play therapists rely heavily on such materials, together with such things as a sand tray in which to use the dolls. For those working with children who have been sexually abused, anatomically correct dolls often prove invaluable. Children can re-enact scenes which are too painful to talk about, or for which they have no vocabulary. Most parents have noted that children like to create figures out of modelling clay. Some child therapists encourage their young clients to do just this. A child can then use a figure as a mouthpiece, and speak the unspeakable.

A related technique is that of using masks. If you have ever watched a child don a mask – and appear to take on a completely different persona before your eyes – then you will be aware of the powerful impact which masks can have on both wearer and viewer. Withdrawn clients, or those struggling with disclosing immense trauma can literally 'hide behind a mask' and adopt another 'self' for the purposes of facing unpalatable or horrendous truths. However the experience of using masks can be *so* powerful that it is generally recommended that therapists do not introduce this work into their practice without specific training and safeguards.

Counsellors working with adults, too, can find great benefit from using dolls and other figures. Human figures for use in therapy can be virtually any size (though anything too huge may prove unwieldy) and, indeed, I like to have a range of sizes available. Over the years I have collected a wide variety of figures – human, animal and fantasy. Some are tiny and can fit easily on a thumbnail while the largest is about as tall as a toddler. Some I have acquired from jumble sales, a few have been bought new, while others are the spoils of raids on my children's toy-box! (If I leave the door of my consulting room ajar when it is not being used, visiting children seem magnetically drawn in there rather than playing elsewhere in the house with my sons' toys. Forbidden fruit? Greener grass? Or just Aladdin's Cave?)

Worry Dolls

A collection of any kind contains items of special interest and I am particularly fond of a set of worry dolls brought back from Arizona by my husband after a recent visit there. He had seen them on sale in large quantities, and recognized them from a set I already possessed, which I had purchased in Canterbury.

At a workshop on creativity in counselling some years ago, I discovered the existence of 'worry dolls' which are tiny, stylized figures hand-made in Guatemala. (Apparently a legend among the highland Indian villagers of Guatemala is that worry dolls will take away worries during sleep. The scrap of paper which came in the box with mine says 'Before going to bed, tell one worry to each doll, then place them beneath your pillow. Whilst you sleep the dolls will take your worries away.' If this smacks of the occult to you, you may choose to avoid these particular dolls. To me, it sounds about as sinister as the tooth fairy.)

On the day of the creative workshop, participants had had a severe shock, having heard a devastating disclosure from a colleague. Working with a partner, I had a choice of various items but felt very much drawn to the worry dolls. 'This is (my colleague),' I said, selecting one doll. I then picked out another doll. Garments of worry dolls are simply a scrap of material wrapped around them. On this doll the material which formed its clothing was beginning to unravel. 'And this is me feeling unravelled,' I went on, which summed up my sense of being taken unawares by what my colleague had said, and feeling out of kilter as I tried to assimilate it. Immediately, I had been enabled, by use of the doll, to express my feeling succinctly. This formed an important stepping stone as I set about exploring those feelings with my partner. Had we relied on verbal means alone, I doubt whether I would have reached the nub of my feeling in the first couple of sentences. Typically, feelings of this sort, which can be hard to describe in the abstract, can be more readily conceptualized when projected onto something tangible.

When inviting clients to work with them I offer a small tray and the box of worry dolls. Most then remove the dolls one at a time from the box (or perhaps tip out the entire contents of the box) and identify some of the dolls as representing themselves or people in their world, and place them at strategic positions on the tray. The small size of worry dolls fits them particularly well for exploring situations involving several people. If necessary, a few dozen could be accommodated on a small tray, although in practice most people work with far smaller numbers at a time. Generally, it is the dynamics of relationships which form the basis of counselling sessions utilizing worry dolls. As a person places each doll on the tray, and takes note of its position relative to the other dolls, he or she 'sees' new things about the relationships which had previously been beneath awareness.

Brenda had been for a job interview and had been hurt and surprised at the reactions of her colleagues, some of whom had seemed relieved that she might soon be leaving the firm. She selected each doll and identified it, then placed it on the tray without a great deal of conscious thought as to its 'correct' placing.

However, when she sat back to take a slightly longer view of the scene, she noticed at once that she had placed the dolls representing her colleagues very close to each other, while the doll which stood for her suddenly looked very isolated. Then she understood better than before the extent to which her colleagues treated her as an outsider.

In chapter eight I described some work that Diane, a lay minister, did with stones. But Diane's presenting problem concerned the outcome of a process of assessment. After months of preparation, she had attended a three-day conference hoping to be recommended for training for Christian ministry. Having responded, on paper and in person, in her usual open style, she felt misunderstood by the selectors, whose final decision was to make a 'conditional' recommendation for training. The 'condition' which Diane had to meet was that she had to receive counselling in order to work through various issues which had emerged during the set of selection interviews. (Needless to say, Diane arrived for her first session with me with a mixture of feelings. This situation, in which someone is virtually 'sent' for counselling is known as a Three-Cornered Contract[1] and can be fraught, as the transference tends to be strong. Indeed, as Diane said to me in retrospect 'I just wanted to dump it all on you. It was your fault, so to speak!')

Diane used several worry dolls, on a tray on her lap, to clarify what had happened and her feelings about it. She picked up each figure and identified it: as herself, as one of three members of the interviewing panel plus its secretary. She placed them in certain positions on the tray and made minor adjustments to them until she felt they adequately represented the scene. We both gazed at it for a few seconds. Before I could ask a general question like 'How does it feel to see this scene set out like this?' she pointed out that the doll representing the sole female member of the panel was lying face up, whereas the others were lying face down. This recognition of her 'inadvertent' (or unconsciously deliberate?) placing of the dolls was sufficient to trigger a vital step in her understanding of the situation. She realized that, while the female member of the panel had responded warmly – she had shown her face – the men had been more distant. It was as though they had hidden their true faces behind the roles they were occupying. This insight helped Diane understand why she had felt that her self-revelations were not treated empathically.

As Diane came to this new awareness, my role was mainly to be present: not just to remain with her in a physical sense but also psychologically and spiritually. While she did not require verbal interventions during this process, she definitely did need to have the memory of *not* being treated empathically softened by an experience of receiving that very thing. Later, my role widened as we drew out the nuggets of learning about what the experience had to offer, and as I helped her consider whether, in anticipation of future interviews, she wanted to adjust her expectations and interview skills.

The small size of worry dolls also makes them very easy to move about. A variety of juxtapositions can be tried remarkably easily. People can be invited to become aware of their different emotional reactions as they move the dolls to form various tableaux. However, the dolls cannot stand, but have to lie, which can be a disadvantage, for example, if a client is ranging figures around a wooden cross. (Though I suppose they could be placed prostrate!)

Worry dolls are ideal for exploring roles, the dynamics of relation-ships and situations involving several people. They are less suitable for people with very large hands or whose fine motor skills are reduced, as those with large or stiff fingers find the dolls hard to manipulate.

When working with people who may find projective techniques threatening, worry dolls are a good choice of tool. While each is indi-vidually made, the colour of the scrap of material forming their cloth-ing is almost their only distinguishing characteristic. Some clients intuitively comprehend the projective aspects of work of this kind and feel very exposed when selecting from among a more varied set of fig-ures whose individuality could prove very revealing. Therefore, once a client has overcome the hurdle of reaching out towards the worry dolls, they are spared a great deal of exposure connected with their specific choices.

Other Human Figures

Two baskets in my counselling room hold a collection of about 50 other figures. (Until recently they were all in one basket but the small-er ones kept dropping to the bottom where they were at risk of being overlooked. I now keep them in two baskets, sorted roughly according to size.) It is usually possible to make use of the same small tray, though I also keep a larger tray available, should it be needed.

Some dolls, like the worry dolls, do not easily stand. Counteracting this problem is one reason why play therapists often employ a sand tray. I keep a box with a few inches of sand in the bottom, and sometimes suggest that people place the figures in it. (In counselling, though, everything is grist to the mill, so the fact that a doll does not remain upright may, for example, give physical expression to the person's per-ception that the person it represents 'doesn't stand on her own two feet', 'backs off when I need him', 'can't be relied upon' and so on.) When travelling to present workshops I substitute sesame seeds for sand. Having similar properties to sand these support the figures in much the same way, but are easier to clear up should they be spilled.

For some pieces of counselling work the choice of worry dolls or these figures seems immaterial, but at other times the figures seem more useful. They consist of all sorts of dolls which I have amassed over the years. They possess (to a far greater degree than do worry dolls) individual characteristics. This tends to increase the extent to which clients treat them as representing real people. I believe it is because of this that people relatively often ask to borrow a figure which they have worked with during one session until the next (a baby doll they have used as their vulnerable or Child part; or a shepherd they have turned into the Good Shepherd, for example). So far no one has asked to borrow a worry doll.

When clients use the figures to personify themselves, or those close to them (their 'significant others') this tends to lead to more dialogue between the figures. That is, the client may enact a conversation between two of the dolls. Sometimes this is a repeat of an actual conversation, used as a springboard into an exploration of the feelings of each of the people represented. (Or, more accurately, of the feelings the client supposes the other people had at the time.) In other situations the conversation is an imaginary one, allowing the person to express what he or she fantasizes about an event or within a relationship.

As most children pass through a stage in which such conversations form an oft-repeated part of their play, its use in therapy tends to be accepted relatively easily by most people, who simply have the experience of returning to an earlier stage of development. Far from being asked or expected to do something threateningly 'new', they are asked to do something which is 'old hat': something they first did around the age of two or three.

Stephen, a computer engineer, used three figures one week. His presenting problem was an aggressive manner at work which his manager believed was likely to lose the company customers, and therefore money.

Stephen worked quickly during sessions, his computing background enabling him to readily appreciate cause and effect. In the first session he was able to identify a frightened, insecure part of himself who tends to lash out rather than risk being attacked by the other person. He gave a very telling word picture: a policeman was trying to keep order between an intimidating 'bovver boy' repeatedly taunting a smaller, weaker lad. The smaller boy continually rushed at the first youth, but came off worse each time.

Such a rich, vibrant picture of his interior world seemed a real treasure and I used it as a stepping stone into a description of Transactional Analysis, especially its notion of ego-states. Stephen returned to this image at the next session, having produced an extremely impressive flow diagram of the process in the meantime. I invited him to arrange a conversation between the three 'people', or ego-states and offered the baskets of figures. He had no trouble choosing a policeman, a little boy and a leather clad, jackbooted figure. In setting up their 'conversation' he brought to the surface some areas of vulnerability in his Child part which he had tended to deny and therefore keep hidden. He was able to strengthen his Adult part who was taking a sensible, reasonable line. And he placated and disempowered his taunting Critical Parent part. Stephen was moving very fast and was fascinated by his new discoveries. He was very pleased to borrow all three figures during that week, and reported later that he had kept them in his pocket so they were often drawn to his attention.

Some uses of dolls can be quick, yet extremely effective. A social worker who comes to me for supervision was recently confused as to the right decision to take, with regard to a child's placement. My knowledge of him as a caring, child-centred man led me to expect that he would give primary consideration to the needs and welfare of the child; yet he seemed to be giving more weight to the wishes of the various adults who were involved. After rummaging around in my basket of dolls, I pulled out a small female figure, held it in front of him and said 'Look at the little girl and tell *her* how you came to your decision.' Immediately he realized that his first concern was her welfare and contentment. This galvanized him into action and he went away to implement a number of changes, based on this renewed commitment to the child in his care.

He returned for his next session, commenting on the power of suddenly being brought up short (which he called being 'gob-smacked'!) and confronted with the child whom he had been discussing. Apparently, he had found that if the focus of his thinking ever started to drift away from the little girl and towards, say, his own professional standing, the image of the doll would float into his consciousness and he would steer his thinking back onto course. I am reminded of instances in which people report that they have been enabled to carry out some very demanding task, or endure gruelling circumstances, by keeping a loved one's face at the forefront of their conscious minds. The interesting contrast here is that it was not the actual child's face that floated in front of my supervisee's eyes, but a doll!

Larger, Soft Toys

Ranged along a shelf and hanging from a chain in my consulting room are several stuffed toys of different kinds and rag dolls of each sex and various ages. One man, after reading about psychosynthesis with its notion of each person having a number of sub-personalities, wanted to spend a counselling session becoming clearer about his own sub-personalities. He elected to use the soft toys and soon the floor was covered with dolls and toys. But he was certainly not playing – at least not in a frivolous way. The right side of his brain was engaged in sorting, checking and re-evaluating elements of his subconscious.

The beauty of creative techniques is that one never knows what will happen or what the route will be. Recently I found myself suggesting something to a client which sounded absurd, if not verging on the blasphemous, yet which proved to be profoundly therapeutic. Having recently participated in some group work in which a group member had taken the role of Jesus, and cradled her while she cried bitterly for all sorts of losses experienced in childhood, she came to her next individual session wanting to develop this further.

At first she tried chair work, imagining Jesus to be on the beanbag and then moving to sit with her back against it, 'cradled' by Him. Kate was frustrated, however; she was desperate to feel the warmth of the Lord's touch but unable to make the imaginative leap required.

Some readers may be wondering why I was reluctant to take the place of Jesus for Kate, and cradle her. In one-to-one work, I very seldom touch clients as I respect the intimacy of touch and do not want to convey confusing messages. (The public nature of group work means that I use touch differently when facilitating a group. There, I may slip an arm round someone's shoulders, for example, with little risk of the gesture being misconstrued. Further, transference tends to be stronger in individual work but diluted in groups – by virtue of being shared – and I believe that for me to have taken the place of Jesus could have strengthened Kate's positive transference to untherapeutic, even unethical levels, by fostering her dependency on me.)

Suddenly I had an idea. Wondering whether it was inspired or mad I suggested to Kate that she pick up a teddy from the shelf and imagine it as herself. Then I suggested that she nurture the teddy as if she were Jesus nurturing herself. Even as Kate lifted the teddy to her cheek and closed her eyes, she visibly relaxed. Her lips parted slightly and she murmured inaudible words of comfort to surrogate-Kate. I could see without a doubt that by projecting herself onto the teddy and drawing on a secure relationship with Jesus to enable her temporarily to act as His stand-in, Kate was finally able to feel herself receive the Lord's compassionate love again.

Again I want to emphasize that, though people may be using toys in the counselling room, they are not 'playing mindlessly' or just for 'fun'. Any 'play' is in the context of a child's 'play' which is sometimes described as a child's work. There may be smiles and even chuckles from clients as they have 'A-ha!' experiences – but nevertheless their purposes are deadly serious. To illustrate this further, I include below a section from Kate's journal, written immediately after the session in which she cuddled the teddy.

As I picked up the teddy bear, I held it instinctively. Immediately I was aware of Jesus, and could feel His presence and His Holy Spirit close to me. I became aware of how tightly I was holding the bear and how much tension there was in my body. I also noticed that my hold on the bear was complete. My arms were completely surrounding it and my hands were holding its feet. My face was resting on its head with my cheek touching its fur. I was cradling the bear against my breast and tummy.

I realized that Jesus was showing me that He wants to hold me tightly but lovingly, so that I can feel safe and secure, and in that security I could (and did) relax. Jesus showed me that although I was relaxing in Him, He was actually quite tense while doing all the 'work' necessary to enable me to relax, taking all my anxieties away.

Jesus loves me so much that He wants to take all my pain away. He wants me to be totally safe in Him, and while He's holding me I will be. Jesus wants to, and is soothing me all over, to reassure me. Jesus wants to and is holding me against His breast, against His heart. Even Jesus' face is against mine, so that He is in total contact with all of my body. He is holding my legs and arms and His cheek rests on my hair.

Whatever position I am in, Jesus can adapt to hold me. He will move to surround me with His body and love. I don't have to be in a particular position for Him to hold me.

Jesus wants to protect me totally from other people's problems and He wants to heal me at the moment. Jesus doesn't want me to worry or be responsible for other people's problems, however closely related or attached to them that I am. I have to leave that responsibility with Jesus. He has shown me through the teddy that all He wants for me is to be whole again.

I'm not sure why, but at this point I put the teddy down on the floor by my feet and considered my feelings as I looked at the teddy on the floor. I felt unhappy and 'cold' being separated from the teddy, and wanted to pick it up quickly. I wanted to go back to the security of holding the teddy, and having Jesus close to me. I picked it up again.

Jesus showed me that He wants me to be in his arms all the time, and He doesn't like it when I go off on my own. It feels uncomfortable to Him. He feels a loss. He wants me to come back to Him. Even though He can find me wherever I am, He wants me to be wanting and looking for him.

I want to remember the tension was in Jesus, taking the tension out of me.

Other people return to the same figure (or figures) session after session. I referred to Pam, who was rather immature, in chapter nine. She still lived with her parents in the quiet, loving home in which she had been brought up. Devoted to Pam, their only child, her parents had tended to cushion her from reality and take decisions on her behalf. Pam recognized that the time had come to loosen the tight links with her parents and told me that she needed to 'grow up'. Taking a history, I perceived a young woman who, though striving to become less dependent on her parents, lacked certain necessary skills.

I outlined for her the basic tenet of Transactional Analysis, that is, that each individual has a Parent, Adult and Child part (or ego-state) and operates in each at different times. We agreed that our task was to strengthen her Adult and Parent parts, so that she could make decisions for herself.

We then embarked on a series of counselling sessions in which she would sit with three soft toys on her lap: a kangaroo with the joey from her pouch held separately, and a rag doll. Pam had chosen these to represent her Parent, Child and Adult ego-stages respectively. Sometimes they were only brought out when the session was well underway; on one occasion, Pam arrived feeling tense and selected the toys before she had even sat down. (Some people work with the same figures over a period of time; one lady makes a grab for a particular soft toy as soon as she enters my room – she calls it her 'security blanket'. Others return to the same figures for several consecutive weeks, exploring relationships from various perspectives.)

Using the three figures, Pam was able to disentangle the reactions of her various ego-states and to learn to select between them to suit the requirements of a particular situation.

At times, she carried out dialogues; for example, between her Parent part who was telling her that she would not be able to survive in the world without help (that is, living anywhere other than in her parents' home), and her Adult part who pointed out the facts about her intelligence, common sense and proven ability to hold down a job and manage her financial affairs. Sometimes the mother kangaroo would hug the baby and reassure her when she was feeling tense or anxious. Initially, this was a demonstration of the attitudes of Pam's ego-states, that is, two parts of herself. At a later stage, though, she began using the figures rather differently. Suddenly the joey was voicing criticisms of the mother kangaroo; these expressed feelings which Pam had about historical events involving her mother.

This fluidity of response is common, and indicates transference, introjection or projection. Here, Pam had introjected (taken into herself) characteristics of her mother which she despised. Initially she responded to them 'as if' they were another part of herself but then shifted gear and began responding instead to their source: her mother.

Using Figures to Explore Transference and Other Psychological Processes

A rule of thumb which I use is that when people show a reaction to a person or event which they (or perhaps I) discern as being stronger than would seem warranted, I take this as a strong indication that some other process is at work. For example, if a man states with considerable feeling that he dislikes a particular woman, I may ask him whether she reminds him of anyone from the past. If this hooks him into strong feelings or memories connected with (typically) his mother, then transference is operating. Or, if a woman complains about some characteristic of another person, such as a boss who is mean or sloppy, I may sensitively point out that statements of that kind often stem from projection, and invite her to identify and own her own meanness or sloppiness. (The principle here is simply the well-known one, that we most hate in other people those features which we hate in ourselves, even though we sometimes deny them in ourselves.)

One middle-aged woman, Jill, whose marriage had been in difficulties for many years, was coming to understand how her unhappy childhood continued to affect her.

I had chosen to describe transference to her by using dolls. I had asked her to choose dolls to represent herself as a child, Peter (her husband), and her parents, which she had done. When I then asked her to select some dolls to represent herself in various current roles I was fascinated to notice that she chose a motherly type, a secretarial type and a fun-loving type, thereby demonstrating her own Parent, Adult and Child ego-states. Together we had moved the dolls into different positions as if 'acting out' certain events. By selective usage of each of the ego-state dolls, and strategic placing of the various dolls, Jill was helped to see the considerable effect which transference was having in her relationship with her husband. For example, one breakthrough came when she placed herself and her husband as if in confrontation, and I moved her little girl-self and father into position directly behind each of the other two. Immediately she could identify with the fact that, often, when she and Peter are in conflict, it *feels* as if she is a little girl being 'told off by Daddy'.

When Jill returned the following week she had barely sat down before she started raking through the baskets of toys to find those she had used the previous week. Apparently a particular incident had occurred which she thought fitted the context we had been considering. We explored it using the dolls and confirmed that her own understanding of what had taken place was indeed correct. At the end of the session Jill borrowed the dolls, saying that she wanted to show them to Peter, and explain to him the dynamics of what had occurred between them.

At the next session she told me that demonstrating with dolls had proved a useful device in communicating the complex dynamics in operation to her husband who has no background in psychology or counselling and so is not familiar with the concepts being postulated.

Puppets
Many counsellors use puppets in their work, and these have many of the features of the figures I have already discussed. However there are some specific points relevant to the use of puppets.

Somehow, puppets seem slightly less threatening to a client than do dolls. I suspect that this has something to do with their having rather different cultural associations: while dolls are for children to play with, puppets can either be used by children, or by adults entertaining them. So people's dignity may seem less affronted when offered puppets to use. Another reason, I suspect, for the slightly greater acceptability of puppets than soft toys and other figures, is that they can be used very close to the body, and so people may feel less exposed.

(On the other hand, most people are willing to use either. As with anything, if the therapist offers them in a confident, unapologetic way, the client is highly likely to accept the suggestion.)

Puppets have been the chosen vehicle in two recent sessions of supervision. In one, the supervisee felt perplexed as to what was going on between himself and his client. Sitting with a puppet on each hand, conducting a dialogue between them and (a vital point) tuning into the feelings of each, he recognized extremely quickly the mismatch between his expectations and those of his client. Instantly he could see the step he needed to take in order to change the dynamic.

In another supervision session, Elizabeth (a counsellor) reported feelings of professional self-doubt, coupled with a belief that 'other counsellors' practise differently – and better – than she. Elizabeth asked to proceed using puppets and chose one to represent herself, and another to represent 'other counsellors'. (Although she was referring to them in the plural, I regarded 'other counsellors' as a composite, so it did not seem necessary to have them represented by more than one puppet. Had she, at any point, discriminated between the members of the group then I would have suggested that she represent them by additional dolls. Also, had she chosen to work with dolls rather than puppets, I would probably have asked which dolls (plural) she was going to choose. However, the floppy nature of hand puppets and their mode d'emploi mean that working with more than two or three at a time is awkward.)

In exploring her modes of practice Elizabeth carried out a short dialogue between the two puppets, with herself claiming not to know 'how to do things properly' and the 'other counsellors' rattling off examples of their own 'good practice'. Even as she proceeded with the dialogue, Elizabeth had a wry smile on her face, indicating that she recognized the irony of claiming not to know how to do something, then immediately putting into the mouth of a puppet words which demonstrated perfectly that she *did* know.

At this point it became clear to her that her own so-called 'inability' to do these things was not in fact inability at all. I then suggested that she introduce another puppet to represent her clients, and check its response to the other two. Immediately she put into the 'clients'' mouths a strong preference for her own brand of empathy rather than the slick, technical expertise of the 'other counsellors'. By now it was evident that Elizabeth had the necessary knowledge and techniques available to her; but that she usually chose to emphasize more her empathic warmth.

In considering the insights she had gained, Elizabeth felt far clearer about the unconscious choices she had made and now valued her own approach considerably more highly than before.

Artefacts and Neutral Items

My collection of objects is not limited to figures but also includes photographs, scaled down artefacts of all kinds, such as doll's house furniture and equipment and neutral items such as scraps of ribbon. In my practice the artefacts are seldom used, though I believe that play therapists may make considerable use of such items. For example, instead of just choosing a doll, it can be placed on a bicycle or in front of a television, signifying the interests of the person it represents.

Neutral items are used more often by those who come to see me. When these are selected they tend to be given symbolic meaning. For example, a piece of card may serve as a barrier between two dolls, indicating the paucity of their communication; or (as in Louise's work described in chapter five) a baby doll may be enveloped in cotton wool, emphasizing its vulnerability or God's protection. On the other hand, artefacts alone can prove useful, for example, when someone is experiencing a block and is unsure what they need to address. At these times, I may offer a person the basket containing 'bits and pieces' and invite them to select any to which they feel drawn, or any by which they feel repelled. A miniature football, selected in these circumstances, uncorked a torrent of hitherto hidden resentments towards a father who, his daughter felt, had preferred football to her.

Counselling Keynotes

Some people take to using dolls and puppets as easily as the proverbial duck takes to water. Others show initial hesitation, but soften after a few moments. Basically, if you are relatively comfortable with the idea (and, of course, have experienced it for yourself) most people will be willing to let you facilitate them. (Anyway, counselling is still such an unknown quantity that people have little idea what to expect and may even anticipate your using slightly wacky methods!)

Be prepared for sudden changes of pace and mood if you incorporate dolls and other figures into your practice. As people begin working with them, their speech tends to slow, indicating that they are switching from left side of brain cognition with its reliance on verbal processes, to right side of brain affect with its penchant for imagery and symbolism.

They often then show sudden flashes of insight or emotion as they get in touch with some of the truths underlying their situation.

Your task is both to 'stay with' the person who is working – and to be aware of what is not being addressed. The notion of 'figure and ground' can be useful here: Elizabeth's 'counsellor' and 'other counsellors' had a dialogue, but needed the 'clients' puppet to show the way through the impasse.

As with any materials, different people use dolls and other figures in different ways. Some carry out dialogues while others concentrate on the proximity of figures to each other; some use them to resolve a situation involving themselves and other people, while others concentrate on the conflicting interests of their own sub-personalities. In common with any creative techniques, unexpected – creative – things often happen. Expect the unexpected!

1. Fanita English, 'The Three-Cornered Contract', in *Transactional Analysis Journal*, Vol. 5, 4, 1975, pp. 202–3.

11

NO MAN IS AN ISLAND

Group Work

Receiving the affirmation which individual counselling offers can make a huge difference to a person's life. Usually life-changing, sometimes life-saving, the impact of that special relationship can hardly be overstated. What, then, is the point of group counselling? Certainly, that is the usual response I receive if ever I suggest that joining a group may be a useful next step for someone I have been seeing for a while.

People find it hard to believe that they could gain any extra benefit from group work. Their objections are generally twofold. For a start, they reason that they currently have my undivided attention and would be reluctant to 'share' therapy time with other members should they join a group. Secondly, people sometimes voice the fact that while they have come to feel comfortable 'baring their souls' to one other person, they anticipate experiencing more inhibitions in a group. It is difficult to dispel these apprehensions in the abstract but many of those to whom I have recommended group work do indeed decide (albeit with some trepidation) to give the notion a try. Without exception they have found the experience worthwhile, therapeutic and broadening in ways which they would never have predicted. In particular, they gain great enrichment from meeting other people on a similar journey of self-discovery to themselves.

Typically, participants discover that in group therapy, a supportive, safe environment is provided. People can experiment with other ways of relating, explore and express their feelings, have their negative beliefs about themselves challenged and replaced with more positive ones, and help provide a similar environment for the others in the group.

'Humbling' and 'stimulating' are usual responses, as is Jenny's comment: 'I knew two of the other people already from my church. But I got to know them far more deeply in those six weeks than ever before. And the rest of the group, who at the outset were strangers to me, became like brothers and sisters within that short time. We knew all sorts of personal, deep, intimate things about each other. But after the group ended I realized that we *didn't* know the ordinary things about each other: hobbies, the details of each other's everyday lives and so on.'

There are many varieties of counselling and therapeutic groups: Encounter, TA, psychoanalytic, psychodrama, Gestalt, assertiveness, bioenergetics...the list could go on and on. Creative therapeutic work in a group setting is the source of great satisfaction to me. When the context is Christian, the 'buzz' can be tremendous. I have seen people take gigantic strides towards wholeness, and changing: if not out of all recognition, then definitely in ways that lead others to comment that they seem 'brighter', 'happier', 'more confident' or 'more in touch with God'.

Group Ground Rules

In my opinion, one hallmark of an ethically established therapeutic group is the existence of ground rules. Certainly it is the ground rules which provide the backdrop against which creativity can occur. These are agreements entered into by all members and the facilitator(s) in the manner of a group contract. They are prescriptive and proscriptive with regard to the behaviour of those in the group and are designed to increase the safety of the group. In the following discussion, references to 'group members' should be taken to refer also to the facilitator(s), unless the context indicates otherwise.

Group members tend to feel extremely vulnerable, especially at the first meeting. Sometimes I invite people to stand on an imaginary line across the room, indicating their current level of fear by their position on the line (with one end standing for 'no fear' and the other end standing for 'extreme fear'). While there is usually a spread of responses, typically there is considerable clustering between the mid-point and 'extreme fear'. Sometimes, people will attempt to demonstrate their own high level of fear by pretending to go *through* the wall or door which marks the end point!

Part of the anxiety which contributes to these feelings of vulnerability stems from questions concerning trust. 'Can I trust these other people?' or 'Are they going to humiliate, exploit or abuse me?' are just two of the many unspoken questions which are probably going through people's minds as they deliberately open themselves to the vulnerability involved in embarking on group work. Establishing ground rules is an essential part of containing these questions.

Ground Rule One: Confidentiality

One of the sources of great uneasiness for members of a therapeutic group concerns confidentiality. People need assurance that personal disclosures will not be spread abroad. There are various levels of confidentiality. At the top level is secrecy about the very existence of the group, which seems more extreme than is necessary or even healthy.

A more usual top level of confidentiality for therapy groups is that while the existence of the group may be freely acknowledged, no details of members' identity or activities may be divulged.

More commonly, though, groups agree to a ground rule of confidentiality which allows members to describe exercises, methods or theoretical material without imparting any personal information about the people in the group which could lead to their being identified. (A useful distinction here is between content and process.) There is a world of difference between a person telling a friend: 'We were working on the theme of rejection and getting in touch with our early experiences of it,' and 'You know Beryl, the one who lives in your road? She was telling us about her horrendous childhood. You'd never think it to look at her but...'

In deciding the limits of confidentiality, it is as well to bear in mind the need which group members frequently have for support as they 'unpack' the wealth of material which membership suddenly throws at them. Some groups allow members to discuss what happens in the group with one other person, such as a therapist, close friend or spouse. In other groups, members agree not to discuss the group even between themselves – apart from during group sessions.

At the other end of the scale from the many varieties of confidentiality is the decision that anything which happens in the group, together with anything that is said, can be used in any setting by members. Needless to say, few people feel ready to expose their most vulnerable selves while knowing that, next time they are queuing in a shop, they may overhear themselves inaccurately discussed by two other people in the queue who 'happened' to hear about them from someone else.

Ground Rule Two: No Violence

Part of a group facilitator's responsibility is to provide a safe setting for group members, so the most important requirement is that members should not be at risk of physical harm. This ground rule does not refer only to blatant damage such as would be caused by someone running amok with a knife, slashing at himself or herself, others, chairs, curtains and so on. It can include the 'violence' which is done when someone demeans someone else, or when people engage in self-destructive acts such as putting themselves down. As with many individual clients, I therefore require that members subscribe to a 'no damage to self, others or the room' contract. While it is true that introducing this as a ground rule can cause a certain amount of uneasiness, establishing it does not have to be done in a 'heavy' way. Furthermore, should there be any cause for concern, it is far better to be able to gently remind someone of this contract, than have to start from scratch and lay down new boundaries when emotions are running high.

Ground Rule Three: Members to Take Responsibility for Themselves

Much of therapy is directed towards encouraging people to take responsibility for their own behaviour, words and – to a certain extent – feelings. Therefore it is appropriate to reinforce this in a ground rule for groups. It refers to people choosing whether to take part in any exercises, sharing or group activity. On the whole I find that almost everyone joins in with practically everything; however, should a particular activity prove a stumbling block for someone, then it is the responsibility of that person to do something about it. If someone has a back problem, for example, he or she may prefer to sit out of some physical activities, or if an exercise has brought up more feelings or memories than a person feels able to state openly, he or she may prefer not to contribute to that part of the group activity. (When setting up this ground rule I usually urge people to use even their non-involvement for their personal growth. Rather than sit and, say, compile a shopping list in their heads, I recommend that they explore their feelings about not taking part, or feelings connected with the material that has surfaced for them.)

Ground Rule Four: Attendance

Commitment to the group is vital. Groups that I run are 'closed': membership is set from the beginning and no new members are admitted during the life of the group. In a group of this kind, even more than an 'open' group, which potentially has more fluid membership, it is especially important that each person can more or less guarantee that the same set of people will be present when the group next meets. It can be disconcerting and frustrating to expose one's deepest insecurities one week, then find that several members of the group fail to attend the following week. A common response would involve a certain degree of self-referent thinking. In other words, the person who had done the 'soul-baring' may feel rejected, and wonder whether other people found the revelation of the person's 'true' self too upsetting or disgusting to bear. Of course, such assumptions (though projections) reinforce the insecurities which the person was trying to overcome in the first place.

Less potentially traumatic, but nevertheless the source of some frustration, is the reappearance of a group member after an absence in which a major revelation has been made. In this case, the jarring may well be experienced by the non-attender, as well as by the one who has revealed traumatic material. The group will have taken a mighty step forward in cohesion and empathy and the person returning will sense this and feel excluded from the intimacy, even if attempts are made to 'update' him or her.

Punctuality is important, too. Starting and finishing at the agreed times provides boundaries which are necessary in any therapeutic work, and establishing a ground rule of punctuality reinforces the value of the group experience, as well as of oneself and the other individuals who share it.

Ground Rule Five: No Observers

Typically, members of groups which I run come from a variety of settings: perhaps they have been students on a counselling course, or clients of mine. Others have simply expressed a desire to participate in a group as they pursue personal growth. Some are counsellors, eager to experience the extra dimension which a group offers, and committed (by their Code of Ethics and Practice, for example) to continuing their personal development. Initially, others attend a group in order to learn about counselling, or say they are keen to deepen their understanding of 'how people tick': but soon find themselves touched at a personal level by the process.

When someone enquiring about group membership expresses an interest in 'learning how people tick' I am always quick to make clear that a therapy group is not a place for observers. It would feel very uncomfortable and possibly demeaning to a person struggling in the public arena (which a group represents) with searingly painful, deeply personal issues, to feel that he or she was being put under the microscope and analysed by a dispassionate onlooker. It would negate, or at least dilute, the tremendously therapeutic benefits which being part of a group offers. It is moving to see the speed with which cohesion occurs, and the deep fellow feeling which exists almost from the beginning of the life of the group. As one person exposes the nature and depth of his or her particular pain, other group members typically demonstrate extremely high levels of empathy. Their support is there, as a backdrop to the person's struggle, as they root for the person and will him or her towards integration.

Further Possible Ground Rules

The ground rules I have listed are fairly standard for group work. However, I have been in groups which have been set up differently, with fewer or more ground rules, or with ground rules which have been agreed by negotiation. Those I have set out I regard as fundamental in that they offer a high degree of protection to group members. Eliminating any of them results in an environment which is less safe, and I regard safety as an essential basic requirement before people will unbend enough to be open to therapy. Other facilitators add further contracts; for example, that no one can attend the group while under the influence of alcohol or 'street' drugs, or that there should be no sex between group members.

Introducing either of these is likely to cause consternation in some settings, including many Christian groups. To prohibit the attendance of members who are on Ecstasy – or to forbid participants seeking ecstasy with each other between sessions – when the life of the group may only be six weeks and is composed mainly of women 'of a certain age' who are stalwarts in their home churches – verges on the ludicrous! (I recall invigilating postgraduate examinations many years ago and having great difficulty quelling an attack of the giggles when solemnly reading the test preamble to the mature students sitting in rows before me. I had to instruct them only to use HB pencils to complete the test forms: 'You may not use pens, felt-tips or *crayons*'! My efforts to steel myself to deliver this message without succumbing to chuckling were nearly wrecked when I caught sight of one student who was clearly tickled by the notion of mature students routinely carrying crayons on their person!)

Some practitioners, perhaps particularly those with a training in Gestalt, add other ground rules relating to features of the verbal communication between members, such as using 'I' rather than 'we all', 'everyone', 'you' or 'one'; or 'no gossiping' which refers to speaking directly *to* a person who is present, rather than talking *about* him or her; and not talking about anyone who is absent.

My own preference is to introduce guidelines on verbal behaviours such as these when they are being broken, rather than add to an already rather formidable list at the beginning of the group. Also, commenting on these behaviours when they have just occurred, means that the circumstances provide an immediate, relevant example, which renders the comments instantly comprehensible. In addition, this method allows group members some say in negotiating whether the group should adopt these guidelines as ground rules, in addition to the non-negotiable ones I had introduced at the outset.

Other ground rules are optional extensions of the compulsory list. You may choose to include, under 'No damage to self, others or the room', behaviour which takes place outside the group but which is related to what happens in it. Driving too fast, taking out uncomfortable feelings on a spouse, child or pet (properly known as displacement behaviour, but often referred to as 'kick the cat'), over-use of alcohol or food – all sorts of activities can be included. The facilitator's role is to weigh up which of these additions or extensions to introduce (and when) so as to ensure the highest levels of safety for group members (and him or herself); but without reducing rapport between the facilitator and the group, by evoking feelings of resentment (at being patronized or 'misjudged') or plain terror!

Contracts

As we have seen, there exists a variety of groups. My own usual pattern is to use warm-ups or just 'doing the rounds' (checking how each individual is feeling) to throw up issues and hence identify a 'protagonist' (or someone 'to work' or 'be in the spotlight' according to your preferred terminology). It is imperative at that stage, though, that the facilitator does not proceed on the basis of an *assumption* that the person wishes to use group time at that moment. When I was training, the phrase 'never counsel without a contract' was impressed upon us, which I consider a tremendously useful motto, as it puts into a nutshell this ethical consideration.

By 'never counselling without a contract' facilitators avoid the risk of exploiting group members by pressuring them to do something they would rather not do: or, to put it another way, they stay in Adult rather than slipping into Parent. It is vital that group members do not have control wrested from them but instead are empowered. This is especially true of people who are depressed or who have been abused.

Some group facilitators (and this is particularly true of TA therapists) draw up contracts with each member when the group is first established. Certainly this helps to provide focus, should proceedings threaten to become 'woolly'. However, there is a price to be paid in terms of curtailment of some spontaneity. Christian groups in particular, seeking to be led by the Holy Spirit, often pursue very different issues and aims – once the process begins – from any which individual members would have included in contracts at the outset.

Group Techniques

As in my individual practice, so also with groups: my approach is eclectic.

I sometimes make use of games or warm-ups from sources such as the *Gamesters' Handbook*,[1,2] or adapted from others I've experienced or made up over the years. Usually I have one or two ideas 'up my sleeve', as it were, but I like to be flexible and respond to the group as it actually is, rather than as I think it may be when I am preparing.

Naturally, a personal growth group functions differently from a therapy group and may rely considerably more heavily on 'games' which as we have seen, can lead to useful insights, despite their name.

While different facilitators approach therapeutic group work in different ways, my preferred approach is based on the psychodrama model and comprises three stages: warming up, action and sharing. Psychodrama involves the resolution of conflicts by acting them out and reversing roles with other group members who play certain parts.

Warming Up

Just as in televising a comedy show, so with a therapeutic group: people may initially be unresponsive and require some introductory activities to help them unbend. 'Warm-ups' or 'starters' are generally used in group work to start the process of unfreezing participants in order that they can derive the most benefit from (and make the greatest contribution to) the group.

While secular groups can benefit from a host of approaches and techniques, a Christian group has the added, huge advantage of being surrendered to the Holy Spirit. An invaluable resource, which can be used openly in Christian groups, is that of prayer. A time of quiet or of verbal prayer at the beginning of a group session, when people wait together to hear from the Lord, allows the Holy Spirit to take charge. Sometimes He gives words, pictures, impressions or a passage from scripture which, when shared with the group, provide the foundation for some personal work by one person. Or, the Holy Spirit may use similar means to reveal a general theme for the session.

Different warm-ups are chosen according to the desired outcome. At the beginning of a group's life, members may not know each other, so some games designed to encourage people to learn each other's names are appropriate. One example is for participants to stand in a circle and take turns throwing a ball across to someone else, while calling out their own name. A variation is to call out the name of the person who is to catch the ball. Other more passive examples can be carried out sitting down. For instance, one person says his name, then his neighbour says both the name of the first person and his own. The third person says all three and so on.

It is worth noting that even such a simple exercise as that can bring up feelings: some people's stress levels rise markedly when it comes to their turn, especially if they have to remember several names. This can relate simply to temperament, in that some people recall names more easily than others. Also, feelings of rejection can be triggered in vulnerable individuals if theirs is the only name that gets forgotten! Asking people to work in pairs is considerably less threatening for most people than relating to the whole group at once. In pairs, people could be asked to discuss how they came to be given their name, and perhaps their feelings about it. Pairs can then join up to form groups of four, and run through the same material, or each person can introduce his or her partner to the whole group, together with the information about the choice of their name.

Other warm-ups may be reflective, such as a guided fantasy or an invitation to people to think back through the week and notice how often, for example, they were aware of feeling angry, apologized, spent time doing something specifically for themselves, or whatever. Or they can be noisy or physical, such as asking participants to move round the room in a particular manner, such as confidently or timidly.

Warm-ups have several important functions, in addition to encouraging members to 'unfreeze'. They can help people to contact their Child ego-state, if that is appropriate, and help them begin to focus on their emotions. Group cohesiveness is encouraged as everyone joins in an introductory task, and many warm-ups put people sufficiently in touch with their interior life that the main piece of work for the session is triggered.

Of course, Christian groups have a whole extra dimension of possible activities. I sometimes read a portion of scripture and ask people to enter into the words as fully as possible. The story of Jesus calming the storm (Luke 8:22–5) for instance, raises questions such as whether people are willing to call out to Him to deal with the storms in their lives; while the story of blind Bartimaus (Luke 18:35–43) lends itself to the suggestion that Jesus may be asking them, too, 'What do you want me to do for you?' (verse 41).

Action

By the end of the warming up period, it is usually becoming obvious whether the evening is to include a major piece of personal work by one individual, or whether the focus is to be more general. During an evening without a specific protagonist, I might introduce 'games' or 'exercises' similar to warm-ups, but which usually require more risk taking, introspection or disclosure: that is, they involve a deeper level of insight or change. For example, the whole group may be invited to give expression to a particular theme which has emerged, such as loneliness or resentment: perhaps by a guided fantasy in which their Child part (who experienced abandonment or loneliness) is nurtured; or by dividing into pairs and taking turns to place (in fantasy) on a beanbag, all the people towards whom they feel resentment, and discharging those feelings.

When I first began facilitating groups their focus was 'personal growth' and a fair proportion of sessions consisted of work such as this. Over the years, though, my approach has evolved and the focus is now usually more firmly that of a therapy group. Now, very few sessions have a general focus (with the exception of the first and often the last meetings of a particular group). Indeed, if any do, I tend to feel that the session has not fully achieved its purpose, and instead has stayed at the 'safe' level of the warm-up rather than deepening in intensity.

While the theoretical model used by the facilitator will affect how a group session begins and ends, almost any group will have a middle section, comprising the main 'work' for the evening. Again, though, the details will vary, with facilitators from different therapeutic approaches using methods appropriate to their training and experience. In psychodrama groups, and usually in Gestalt groups, the session will focus on one main person, whereas in a TA setting, or one which concentrates on group process, input may come from anyone in the group, and attention will shift accordingly.

Examples of a clear protagonist

1 Lisa

Lisa, a married woman in her thirties, had been in personal therapy with me and had now joined a Christian therapy group. In one session, the warm-up had put Lisa in touch with angry feelings towards her father who had physically abused her. She sat, her hands twisting in her lap, her breathing noisy, deep and fast. When I asked if she wanted to work, she said she didn't know; that other people probably had more important needs at that moment. I took these replies to be indicative of her having temporarily regressed to childhood and, in turn, statements of her fundamental beliefs of her Child as being someone who doesn't matter, who mustn't call attention to herself.

This, then, was a tricky moment. As yet we had no contract to work. While Lisa's verbal and non-verbal messages were contradictory, I believed that her healthy inner self wanted to work. Yet it would have been unethical for me to make any attempt to coerce Lisa into the protagonist role. Moreover, to have done so would have been to further abuse her by wresting out of her hands the right to make her own decisions and to keep control of what happens to her. I chose to reflect on what I was seeing and hearing, and the mismatch I had observed. I also dealt with her surface-level objection by inviting her to look round the group and check with each member whether any of them were wanting and ready to work at that moment. None were; in replying, some expressed the desire for Lisa to gain what she needed by taking group time. (In TA terms, 'giving permission' to work or to change, for example, is recognized as a powerful therapeutic element.) By addressing Lisa's Adult in these ways I contacted the part of her which could decide whether to work, and she was able to enter into a clear contract to do so. She said she wanted to 'get rid of' the anger she was feeling towards her father.

The moment-by-moment decisions which I made, from the end of the warm-up onwards, were many. Creative facilitation consists of constantly and silently considering options and assessing which approach is most likely to bring about the desired (and contracted) outcome.

To begin with, I could have invited Lisa to 'put her father on the chair' or to 'be (her) anger'. I could have handed her something (I use a strong, rubber, dog's plaything in a figure-of-eight shape) to exaggerate the twisting of her hands and externalize her anger, or I could have asked her to emphasize her breathing pattern and to allow sounds or words to come as she breathed out. Any of these approaches would have been acceptable, and are likely to have resulted in the cathartic release Lisa needed.

However, any of them could also have been used in individual therapy, as they make no use of the other group members apart from as a supportive presence. While I do sometimes use these methods in group work, I more usually utilize methods which involve other members of the group, in order to increase the sense of participation in each other's work and of aiding each other's healing.

Questioning Lisa, I established that she had 'returned' to her parents' bedroom: that is, while managing to conduct a laboured conversation with me, and stay – at least to a certain extent – in present reality, it was also as if she was a small vulnerable child.

When I asked her how old she felt at that moment she answered, in a small voice, 'Four.' Already I had slowed the pace of my speech to take account of the effort Lisa was making to straddle both worlds. Now I also adjusted my vocabulary and syntax, to ensure that I would be understood by her four-year-old Child part.

I took Lisa's hand and she got slowly to her feet. We started walking slowly round the floor-space of the group as Lisa described the memories which had surfaced. Movement helps people to get (or stay) in touch with emotion. We feel with our bodies, so body movement enhances the experience: you have probably noticed feeling more vibrant and fully alive while walking than when sitting in a chair. Once I considered that I had a feel for the events she was remembering I encouraged her to 'set the scene'. A doll was clearly figural in this memory, so she chose one from a selection of toys that I had brought. It is important that the protagonist leads in scene setting as this encourages the person to 'own' the scene more fully and is an antidote to passivity and dependence on others for things which are, in fact, within the person's own power.

I ascertained that Lisa and her father were the only people present, but that her nuclear family also contained a brother, Steven, who was at school at the time, and their mother, who was at work. (There did not seem to be other influential people whom we needed to take account of, such as grandparents.) With some encouragement, Lisa selected people from the group to play these parts. Clearly only Father was going to be needed immediately, but it is useful to have had the protagonist identify other significant people *before* the action starts, as choosing them later may well not be practicable as it causes too much disruption to the flow of what is happening.

I suspected that, if Lisa were to have begun by playing the scene as her four-year-old self, her rage may have evaporated into fear when faced anew with her abuser. This would have resulted in her 'freezing': being unable to confront him or vent her feelings, and therefore having had her terror reinforced. I therefore asked her to choose someone to play the part of herself: her 'double'. I asked Lisa to place Father and Lisa in their appropriate positions and, standing close to each in turn, to provide their lines and actions.

The major part of the action was short. Lisa was playing on the floor with her doll. Her father told her to play elsewhere. Engrossed, she ignored him, so he roared at her, pulled her up by her hair then tried to stuff the doll into her mouth to stop her crying.

The group members, including Lisa, were sufficiently in touch with their Adult selves for me to feel comfortable asking them to enact this scene. I trusted them to work within the ground rule of 'no harm'. Had I had any misgivings, I would have directed Lisa's work differently – such as using just a selection of toys to represent the people, or reverting to chair work.

Now the action could begin in earnest. I held Lisa's hand and together we stood and watched the scene unfold. I felt her shake as she watched her father drag her double up from the floor. As he began stuffing the doll into her mouth I asked Lisa if she wanted to do anything about what she was seeing. With that she flew across the room shrieking at him to stop. With all her strength she pulled her father off the little girl and I turned her slightly to direct her many blows to a large, strategically placed beanbag. Through tears and shouts, despair and threats, Lisa pummelled for several minutes. Finally she sat back on her heels, drained. Her eyes, though red and tear-stained, now had a light in them which they had previously lacked.

Lisa blinked a few times, as if making an effort to recognize her surroundings. Before she came back fully into the 'here and now' I asked if she wanted to do anything for four-year-old Lisa. Lisa went over to her double, sat beside her and, putting her arms round her, told her what a lovely child she was. She described her character, accomplishments and looks in warm terms, then quietly sang her a soothing lullaby.

After Lisa had enjoyed nurturing herself in this way, I asked her to change places with her double and for the double to repeat the things Lisa had done, said and sung.

A working session like this is exhausting yet exhilarating for all those involved. When everyone had returned to their seats, Lisa needed to spend some minutes talking about the things her father had done to her, and which she had pushed to the back of her mind. Suddenly the memories were crowding in on her and it was important for her to disclose them in the safety of the group. Of major importance, too, was the debriefing and deroling of the group members who had played Father and young Lisa. It is possible for group members who have played certain roles to get 'stuck' in them, or for others to remain 'stuck' in their perception of those who have taken certain roles.

To feel oneself trapped in a different persona can be a terrifying experience, and it is the responsibility of the facilitator to make every effort to ease group members back into their own skins. It can also be very damaging to the relationships within the group if one member becomes permanently cast as, for example, a bully, rapist or delinquent.

In this case, I was concerned about the possibility that negative transference would render the member who had played Father unpopular in the group, so I held his hand and took him to each participant in turn. To each he told his name and a sentence about himself. It was imperative that Lisa and the group member who had played her father re-established their relationship as themselves. They did this by finding the similarities and differences between the real person and the role; and – for Lisa – between 'then' and 'now'.

2 Kim

Kim, a young woman who has been in counselling with me for about three months, recently attended a group I ran. She keeps a journal and has given me permission to reproduce here her journal entry relating to the first group session. For this book she has added a few comments in square brackets to clarify what was happening.

All day I have found it very difficult to reach the Lord in prayer. I have felt a long way off from God when praying. I feel very apprehensive about tonight – the first group session ever for me, and the first for this new group of people. It was hard opening up to Althea when I first started my counselling. I have been wondering what it is going to be like opening up in front of a group of five or seven people whom I have never met before. I have prayed today asking the Lord to prepare me for whatever He wants of me this evening. Whatever happens I know He is in control, and no matter how 'it' makes me feel I know that I can put my complete trust in God. I have also prayed that God will help me be quiet tonight, and not to take over the meeting; that God will help me be sensitive to other people's needs, so that I only speak when appropriate.

As we all meet for the first time, we sit in an intimate circle of chairs around a carpet. There are six of us and Althea. We discuss what the ground rules of the sessions might be. Confidentiality is a key to developing our trust in the group, but to what extent does that confidentiality extend? I feel happy that members of the group can discuss the evenings with a named person, both their experiences and mine. Other members feel that they would be happier only discussing their own material, so that others would not be able to discuss things concerning them. This is what we agree on. We can discuss our own experiences outside the group, but not those of others. I suggest that, in addition, there may be particularly distressing experiences happening to others that affect us, and that at the time we may be able to agree that in that instance, a discussion release valve may be permitted. We agree.

We all introduce ourselves to the other members, explaining who has been to previous groups (there have been two). We give brief explanations of why we are there. My turn comes and I am still apprehensive, wondering what is to follow the preamble. I feel close to tears as I start to speak. I say that I am currently 'knee-deep' in counselling with Althea, and that I will probably be the first in the group to cry as I am close to tears now. They all laugh and say that Althea always has a big box of tissues handy! They have, in effect, said that my tears will be OK and that others have gone before me! I share my concerns as to how easy or difficult I might find these sessions. As we have gone round, I am surprised that three members have been to previous sessions, and are coming back for more – and that they have been on a previous 'learning to counsel' course run by Althea. I am also surprised that a minister is amongst us, but on reflection realize that ministers give of themselves more than most, and therefore from time to time need to receive help themselves.

We start the session with a prayer. Althea leads, asking God to come amongst us by His Holy Spirit and to lead us. That we may respond to what is on His agenda for the evening, and that by words, pictures, emotions or by physical feelings He might show some or one of us what is relevant to this evening. During the prayer, I am waiting on God, wondering what this time of prayer will bring, and whether the Lord will reveal anything to me. I am expectant.

At the end of praying, Althea asks if anyone experienced anything during the time of prayer. Gill says she has seen a picture.

There is a fast moving river, with muddy banks. Someone is standing at the edge trying desperately to dislodge a huge log that is jutting out into the river. The end of the log is all tangled up with weeds, and it is these that are holding the log fast. The person is trying to pull and lever the log free. It is stuck fast.

As she describes the picture something inside me clicks, but this is not a scene from my life. I keep quiet when Althea asks if this picture means anything to anyone, and I also want to give everyone else a chance to respond. No one does. We then go round the group to see if God revealed anything else during the time of prayer. He didn't. Althea is about to go onto something else when I realize that the picture was for me. I take the plunge and have to speak up...

I think the picture could belong to me. The log represents all the things and tasks in my life that I see need doing. I take responsibility for them, hang onto them and then try to deal with them. The river rushing past is the speed of my life going on around me. The bank is muddy and represents the ground

I'm standing on: it is unsafe and can't hold me indefinitely. There is futility in the fact that I'm trying to move the log. I have set this as a goal when I picked up the log, and I have to achieve the task – in my own strength.

Althea suggests that we act out the scene, and asks me if there is anything in the room that I think could represent the log. [One end of the hall has been laid out for the next day's playgroup meeting.] I select a slide hooked onto a climbing frame in the room to act as the log. We all go over to the slide and Althea suggests that I position the slide so that I am happy it resembles the position of the log. I struggle to remove the slide and put it in a suitable position. We discuss the position of the log amongst us; my understanding of the position of the log is different to Gill's who had been given the picture. I am aware that I am going to need to pull the 'log' with considerable effort, and that it needs to resist to enable me to re-enact the scene. As I place the slide, I can see that the climbing frame and the slide are not going to be secure. I am not sure how to solve this problem. I am completely oblivious to the fact that there are people here who could help me! Althea can see me struggling, and comes and puts her arm around me. She reminds me that it is OK to ask for help. I ask the group to hold the climbing frame, thus stopping it sliding across the floor, while I pull the slide as if it were the log. I pull the slide, trying to wiggle it free, but the hooks on the underside of the slide hold it fast. I realize the futility of pulling it now that I know it is stuck.

Althea suggests that I now pretend to be the log. I lie on the floor on my back with my legs stretched out. My head is close to the climbing frame and I hold onto it with my hands. As I lie on the floor holding on with all my strength to the climbing frame, two members of the group pretend to be me pulling the log. Each of them pulls one of my legs. There is no way I want them to pull me free, and they do not succeed. We stop, and talk about what was happening. They admit they were pulling very hard, and were surprised at my tenacity. I describe what it felt like to be pulled: the pulling and tension is coming from my hands, not my legs; the strength is in what was holding the log, so pulling the other end is useless. (Yet in my vision I had kept on pulling, determined that because I had set myself the task, I should and would complete it. On my own.)

As we talk I am aware that my legs have started to tremble. Althea has also noticed, and puts her hand gently on my tummy and asks me to let the shaking come. My legs begin to shake a lot and I think other parts of me are trembling too. [My hands are clenched beside my head, and my posture resembles that of a baby.] Althea suggests that I call out for Mummy. I do, and hardly get the word out before I am overcome with huge sobs, crying from the heart. I roll from my back onto my side, I am making a lot of noise and my hands are shaking uncontrollably. I do not know what to do with them, or where to put them, and I tell Althea. She asks me if I want someone to hold them and I reply 'Yes.' As Althea holds my hands I calm down, I stop crying and my legs stop shaking. I feel safety and warmth from the hands but not love, which surprises me as I assume the hands might be representing Jesus' hands. [I later realize that they were my Mother's, or someone looking after me in her place, and that was why I was crying out for her.]

Althea asks me what would it feel like if Jesus were to hold me, and I reply that it would be nice. She asks me to choose someone from the group to represent Jesus. I know the person I choose has to feel cosy and strong, so they cannot be too slim or small. The choice comes down to two from the group, but I have reservations about both of them. I am quiet for a long time as I consider the options. Althea asks whether I would like the group to make the decision but I know that I have to make it. I reflect my reservations about my two candidates to the group. One of them is male and I am concerned that the hold might feel sexual. The other is a woman I know and I am not sure I want someone I know to represent Jesus. My legs start shaking again, and I know that God is in this decision with me. I feel that the choice has to be Peter, whatever my reservations. As I am making this decision my legs are shaking more. I tell the group that

I would like Peter to represent Jesus, and immediately feel a slight release.

I sit up, still with my eyes closed, and Peter comes and sits close to me and holds me, but I know that this does not yet feel right. I say that I would like to be held from behind with his arms around me, so my head can rest on his shoulder and my back against his arm. I sit back with my legs stretched out and lean into his body, the top half of my body feels completely enclosed, safe and calm in Jesus. I am not relaxed yet.

I realize that my legs won't stop shaking, and that they do not feel at all safe. It's as if my legs and feet do not know what to do with themselves. I tell the group what I'm feeling. Althea asks if I would like someone to hold my legs as well. I have realized that my legs need holding too, not holding down, just holding. I say, 'Yes.' Two people from the group hold my thigh on one leg and my foot on the other leg. My legs have stopped shaking now, they are still but remain tense. They feel secure and supported now. They are not 'wandering' in an unknowing direction.

My whole body feels safe and contained now. Jesus is in total control of my external body. I know that I must ask God to keep me as safe as this and to take control in everything I do, before I do it. In the busy moments of my life, I always try to do things in my own strength first. I don't even think of Jesus, yet I know that God is my rock, and it's Him that has got me this far. So why do I keep forgetting Him? I am troubled because I know what I should do, but do not know how to achieve it. In my prayerful moments I always ask God to guide me, yet I keep closing my mind to Him in the busyness of my life. I really want to be open to Him all the time. I know it's me losing touch with God, and not the other way round. The solution is easy, but how to achieve it seems like a huge mountain in front of me.

Althea asks me what Jesus would like me to do now. I don't know, so she suggests that I ask Him. I pray to Jesus, and as I do I feel a twinge in my foot as it relaxes, and I know that He wants me to relax in Him. I ask Jesus to help me relax. My whole body starts to relax and I rest in Jesus. I feel completely at ease. There are thoughts drifting through my head, but they don't concern me. This is unusual, as normally I would be processing them all. It is a wonderful feeling that I don't have to be in control of this moment – Jesus is taking care of everything.

I'm not even aware of all the problems I was trying to solve five minutes earlier. It doesn't matter how I'm going to solve them, because right now I'm safe with my Lord, and He is in total control. Anyway, it's not going to be me who solves the problems, because Jesus is going to do it for me, and He's not bothered about those right now, so why should I be? I need to trust Jesus as completely as this in everything I do. I need to ask Him to help me. The main thing is not to try to solve the next bit before I've sorted this bit – well, Jesus and I have sorted out this bit. [I am unaware of how much time has passed, but in fact this evening's session is coming to an end.] Althea says we have to prepare to finish now and that as I get up, I might ask 'Jesus' [Peter] to help me put the slide back where it was!

I sit up and ask 'Jesus' to help me put the slide back, as it was before I pretended to be the log. We do so. Althea suggests that I re-enact the original task. This time I'm going to ask 'Jesus' to help me pull the log. I pick up the log first and then start to ask 'Jesus' for help, realizing that I should not even have begun the task without calling on him. Before I *actually do* anything I should ask Jesus for help. I ask 'Jesus' [Peter] to pull the log. Immediately I stand up and lift the log. Althea asks me what 'Jesus' said, and I realize that I have not given 'Jesus' time to say anything or do anything to help me – I did not wait on his answer. Here I am enacting my very fears from earlier in the session – I must hesitate before each task, have patience and wait on the Lord for His help. I put the log back down onto the floor. We all laugh as I realize what I am doing and I think it breaks some of the tension.

Althea suggests that I now represent Jesus. Peter goes to take the log pretending to be me and says what he thinks Jesus would say to me. He asks me to stand behind him while he pulls the log, so that Jesus can help him pull and his footing will be secure. I go and stand behind him as Jesus might have done and put my arms around his waist. This does not feel right, so I tell the group that I do not think that this is what Jesus would say. Althea asks me to go and stand back by the climbing frame, take the part of Jesus and say what I think He would say.

I think Jesus would say that I don't have to do anything with the log, that the log can stay in the water, that it doesn't have to be removed.

We swap places again; I am myself and Peter is back being Jesus. He tells me very sincerely what I think Jesus would say:

'I don't want you to pull this log out. It's OK to leave a job undone. It's OK not to complete or do a job that you see and think needs doing. You have to trust me that I will do the job if it needs doing, even though you are unaware who I may get to do it or when that might be.'

Althea has been close to me as I have been sitting on the floor by the slide, with 'Jesus' by my side. She pats me on the back and says what a brilliant piece of work. At the time I am pleased that she has said that, but don't really understand why, as really it has not been much of me, but more of God and the group.

We all go back to our seats, and discuss how each of us is feeling. As I walk, my legs feel very heavy.

Althea asks me first how I feel, and whether I am fully 'back with the group'. I say that I still feel very heavy-headed, as if the Lord is still working within me. I am puzzled as to what message I am getting about my babyhood and crying out for my Mummy. I can relate to wanting my Mother all through my life, and due to circumstances she has not been there (for example, while I was away at boarding school, while I was pregnant with my two children and now while they are growing up and we are living 70 miles apart).

[In a subsequent counselling session with Althea, we discussed how old she thought I may have been when 'crying out for Mummy'. Althea suggested that from my body posture and hand positions, I was probably about three months old. I remembered my Mum having told me previously that she had had breast abscesses when I was a baby, and had had to be taken into hospital at a moment's notice. Whereupon my Dad had taken me 'lock, stock and barrel' to my maternal Gran and left me there to be looked after. I realize now that not only did I have to contend with the shock of my Mum's 'disappearance', but also that I was suddenly bottle fed instead of breast fed.

During discussions with my Mum at a later date, we realized that this 'crying out for Mummy' was very probably this incident that had happened when I was three months old. I now realize why I had felt warmth and safety from the hands holding me during the group session, but not love. My Gran's cuddles and nurturing would have made me feel safe and warm but at that time Gran and I would not have formed the 'love bond' that is there now. She may well have been giving me all the love that she had for me, but she wasn't my Mum with whom I would already have formed a 'love bond'. Gran has often told me that I was 'special' to her and Gramps, because they had looked after me when I was so young.]

I am astounded that the whole session has been taken up with me, but do not disclose this. We have only known each other as a group for two hours, and yet I already feel very close to everyone. I am immensely grateful to them all for the love they have shown me in the last couple of hours, and the compassion they are feeling now. As we go around the group, everyone is thanking me for how my experiences have also managed to touch them in some way. What a great and mighty God we have, He can use us even in our pain and our learning to help others. No experience is wasted by Him. I feel humbled that I am also receiving thanks, when I feel it is me that owes so much.

As we share, members of the group give me other bits of the picture. For example, that at the middle of a storm or tornado, there is always a still centre. In the busyness of my life, I can turn inwards and find Jesus. He is always there, ready to bring peace and calm – He is my still centre. I just have to look for Jesus and I can rest in His peace. Also, that Jesus is all around us – 'behind us and before' (Psalm 139). This means a lot to me as Althea and I had been talking about praying on the armour of God only a few days before (Ephesians 6:10–20). I always try and approach Jesus face to face. Today I have learnt that maybe I need to ask Him to come and put His arms around me from behind, so I can lean on Him, and allow Him:

- to hold me physically
- to hold me in my Faith
- to hold me up as the water rushes past
- to hold me, so I can rest in him.

Althea finds Psalm 139 in her Bible and hands it to me, asking if I know it. I don't. I feel I should read it now, and ask the group if I should read aloud. They agree. As I read, many of the words go straight to my heart.

O Lord, you have searched me and you know me.
You know when I sit and when I rise; you perceive my thoughts from
afar.
You discern my going out and my lying down; you are familiar with all
my ways.
Before a word is on my tongue you know it completely, O Lord.
You hem me in — behind and before; you have laid your hand upon me.
Such knowledge is too wonderful for me, too lofty for me to attain.
Where can I go from your Spirit? Where can I flee from your presence?
If I go up to the heavens, you are there; if I make my bed in the depths,
you are there.
If I rise on the wings of the dawn, if I settle on the far side of the sea,
even there your hand will guide me, your right hand will hold me fast.
If I say, 'Surely the darkness will hide me and the light become night
around me,'
even the darkness will not be dark to you; the night will shine like the
day, for darkness is as light to you.
For you created my inmost being; you knit me together in my
mother's womb.
I praise you because I am fearfully and wonderfully made; your works
are wonderful, I know that full well.

My frame was not hidden from you when I was made in the secret place.

When I was woven together in the depths of the earth, your eyes saw my unformed body.

All the days ordained for me were written in your book before one of them came to be.

How precious to me are your thoughts, O God! How vast is the sum of them!

Were I to count them, they would outnumber the grains of sand.

When I awake, I am still with you.

If only you would slay the wicked, O God! Away from me, you bloodthirsty men!

They speak of you with evil intent; your adversaries misuse your name.

Do I not hate those who hate you, O Lord, and abhor those who rise up against you?

I have nothing but hatred for them; I count them my enemies.

Search me, O God, and know my heart; test me and know my anxious thoughts.

See if there is any offensive way in me, and lead me in the way everlasting.

Thank you, Lord, that words written so long ago can mean and apply so much in my life today. Amen.

Sharing

Observing another person's work, and perhaps taking part in some way, can be emotionally draining. At the simplest level we can identify with any piece of work, if only through our shared humanity. However different the other person's situation or personality may be from our own, we can always find some points of contact and therefore some degree of empathy.

Other pieces of work may move some people very deeply: there is a sense in which several group members, apart from the protagonist, may be 'working' at once, in that memories may be surfacing, insights may be flowing, connections may be being perceived or emotions may be being catharted. It is therefore in the interests of *all* group members to finish with a time of sharing, debriefing, deroling and perhaps relaxation.

It is essential that anyone who has taken on a role (such as the protagonist's mother or boss) is helped to come completely out of that role and back into their own skin. Failure to derole a person can result in them feeling dazed, zombie-like and out of kilter with themselves and other people. Root each person back in present reality, such as by asking them to state their own biographical details ('I'm Julie Simkins. I'm 38 and I'm married to Joe. We have three children'). Establishing eye contact with each person present is often very useful, and some people need to make physical contact with everyone, too. It can be necessary to root a person back in the 'here and now' by asking them to look at and describe their clothes, or count the number of window panes in the room.

Once fully 'back', each person can be given the opportunity to share with the group the reactions they had as the work unfolded. The protagonist should be invited to go first. As other people comment on the work, it is usual to instruct them to speak directly to the protagonist. It is sometimes necessary to remind them to speak about *themselves*, and not to ask questions or make statements which probe the *protagonist's* mind, attitudes, behaviour or feelings. That is, 'Watching you work took me back to how I was with my mother before she died...' is permissible; 'But don't you think your mother just wanted to teach you right from wrong?' is not.

Counselling Keynotes

Christian group work is perhaps the arena in which the most creative therapy can take place. Secular group work can be very stimulating, but facilitation which is empowered by the Holy Spirit renders it even more creative, growth-enhancing and exciting.

I do not recommend that you try your hand at group work without some training in it, but if you have already studied group dynamics and counselling and wish to broaden the range of your techniques, then you could experiment with using some of the creative materials such as stones or dolls with groups of people.

Alternatively, a personal growth group may evolve out of a previously existing meeting such as a house group. In that case you may want to use guided imaginative prayer, or even techniques from drama therapy to aid the transition. But do be aware of the importance of contracts and informed consent: beware of letting one kind of meeting slide into a different kind without making explicit such things as its identity and aims. Those attending a group which is undergoing transformation need specific opportunities to 'opt in' or 'opt out' when its structure, content and purpose are evolving from those which pertained when they first joined.

It is probably in group work that counsellors run most risk of falling prey to the temptation to 'show off'. The powerful influence of transference means that group members invest the facilitator with great power. (This is true in individual counselling, of course, but in groups the effect can be magnified). Supervision is at least as important here as for other therapeutic endeavours: perhaps more so.

1. Donna Brandes and Howard Phillips, *Gamesters' Handbook*, Hutchinson, 1978.

2. Donna Brandes, *Gamesters' Handbook Two*, Hutchinson, 1982.

Part Three

12

PUTTING IT ALL TOGETHER

In this chapter and the next I will present some examples of working with people in a variety of ways. I mentioned earlier the artificiality of compartmentalizing different methods. The nature of counselling is dynamic and fluid, making it impossible to plan woodenly: 'this week, dolls; next week, stones'. For simplicity I have presented material in that way in the earlier chapters, but in these two chapters I hope to breathe life into the on-going process of counselling and display some of its richness and depth. There are times when the process has something in common with taking a ride on a roller coaster: one encounters dramatic highs and lows; while their occurrence may be expected, nevertheless their timing can be unpredictable. Working with another human being who is travelling to these heights and depths is an immense privilege. I feel I have shared some peak experiences with my clients and I thank God for choosing to use me in this way.

In these two chapters, two of the people I have worked with describe their experience of being counselled and I present two others at some length. To all four I extend my gratitude and appreciation. I believe that these chapters reveal the reality of the *process* of counselling, and of moving between different methods, and therefore add something of great value. One reason for choosing these four people in particular is that, in addition to each being very different from the others and dealing with very different material, the length of time during which they received counselling also varied. Tace was seeing me for over a year, Brenda just came for four sessions, Keith came for 14 sessions, and Katie has been coming for several months.

Case Study 1: Tace (One Year)

Part 1: Tace's Observations

During my time in therapy I kept a journal. Putting my thoughts on paper after the sessions helped me to clarify the work we were doing; it also meant that I got much more than an hour out of each hourly session.

Now, as I look back, I see that I made many changes to my life in this past year. I set out in search of who I really am: in therapy I found I had some choice in being the person I am today.

I am 47 years old, a wife and a mother. I work on a part-time basis, I'm a part-time student and I paint pictures.

I prefer not to disclose my real name so I shall call myself Tace, a choice that is significant to my progress through therapy as the journal will reveal.

Pre-Therapy

One of the myths which developed in my childhood was the belief that nobody was going to take care of me as well as I take care of myself. I was disowned by my parents at 18 years of age and at that time struggled through some difficult years. Consequently I constructed powerful mechanisms of self-defence. I saw therapy, like religion, as a crutch for those who were weaker than myself.

Another of my myths maintained a belief that people were either creative or academic. I am creative, therefore I have no academic ability. In recent years I have challenged this second myth, and in doing so it was necessary to also abandon myth number one. I could not sort out my ideas alone; I needed to see myself from the outside. Therapy offered this opportunity.

Part 2: Tace's Journal

October 1994

Our first meeting was arranged on the telephone – 30 minutes; no fee, no obligations on either side. It was just to see if we both felt we would like to work together.

Althea's room is cosy; like an Aladdin's Cave. I always discover a new treasure. That first time my eyes were drawn to a wooden cross that stands in the window. My understanding had been that religious emblems, like family photographs, were taboo in the counselling room. The atmosphere gave me comfort. There was relief from the implication that my therapist was a real human being, she doesn't hide behind a professional mask.

Session 1: 3 November 1994
I didn't come out feeling good. I suppose first sessions have to be structured around getting information. Maybe I was expecting too much. I had never discussed my personal life with a stranger before. Answering questions was difficult – not because I was holding back but more because this was a first time experience and I didn't know how to do it.

So next week I'll go right back and tell her that our first session wasn't what I had expected and I didn't feel comfortable with it.

Session 2: 9 November 11.30 am
I went in with my notes on last week's session. Being the one with pen and paper in my hand somehow put me in control. Althea was listening and nodding to all my remarks. Then she asked quite gently, 'So what's going on now between us?'

I had slipped into a behaviour pattern that I always feel embarrassed about after the event. It happens like changing gear in a car. I was playing games. I identified the 'imp' – the subpersonality I use for this particular game. Now that he's come into the open I've named him Puck.

Althea pulled the beanbag forward and I willingly moved onto it as Puck, leaving Tace in my original chair. I am surprised how easy it was to feel being Puck. I soon realized Puck was hearing what he wanted to hear rather than what was actually being said.

Althea was in the middle, like a tennis umpire, aware of every move. I was surprised to learn that Puck was on my side, he was doing all this to help me. It seemed he was trying to protect me in the only way he knew. Puck was surprised that I had a rather soft spot for him. OK, his games were not as helpful as he had intended them to be – but there were other sides to Puck. He didn't always have to be an embarrassment. These other aspects seemed to fit into other corners of my whole. Other subpersonalities could use Puck creatively.

He was happy when I put this suggestion to him. I felt so relieved at finding a solution to my internal conflict that I wanted to jump up and down and clap my hands, but some other subpersonality (was this my Critical Parent?) poured cold water on that idea.

Then Althea produced a tray full of 'little people' so that I could choose a symbol to reinforce what had happened. I rummaged through looking for a fairy, but then I found Snow White. A character from the imagination of a creative writer. In a moment Puck was transformed. He is now a positive and valued addition to my creative abilities.

17 November

We seem to be working in a pattern. Althea always checks out at the beginning of a session what I want to work on, so on my drive over I try to work out an agenda. I've also noticed a pattern in the way that frequently I end up talking about my relationship with my mother. I'm still searching around for presenting problems. What I really want to know is who is the real me? Am I really free? Am I missing anything? What do I want to get out of therapy?

Perhaps Althea is asking that question too. That would be why she asks me what I want to work on. Maybe I'm avoiding something. If I am, I am not doing it consciously.

My relationship with Althea is very relevant to what's going on. I started off trying to impress her. Now I just want her to understand me. I guess that goes back to the fact that my mother didn't.

Therapy is a bit like getting a second go at being a child. It's a wonderful opportunity to retrace the foundations of my life. I'm testing things out. I've had a go at being naughty – and I didn't get thrown out. But I'm not sure how Althea is going to be able to understand me when I don't really understand myself. Am I a brainless artist? Or do I have more intellectual ability than I choose to acknowledge? For the time being I'll continue to use Althea's room as my very own toy cupboard and we'll wait and see what happens!

December 1994

My car was frozen and wouldn't start. I couldn't get to my therapy session. First I was disappointed. Then I decided that I didn't need therapy anyway. (It's wonderful how my thoughts work in a way in which I protect myself from disappointment.)

Anyway, I went for a long walk through the beautiful frost-tipped countryside and I genuinely felt that the experience had been more beneficial than my session.

Late December 1994

I wondered if my time would be better spent walking in the woods again. As it happens, I'm delighted I didn't miss this session. I played with 'little people'. We started with me in my first family and I chose little dolls to represent my mother and father. At the same time I was talking about how naughty I was as a small child and how unpopular was my habit of getting into my parents' bed early in the morning. I wasn't really thinking about what I was saying – just sort of reminiscing past times.

Then Althea said, 'You said when you were a baby you were very cruel to your mother. I wonder what makes you say that?' I was surprised. Did I say I was cruel? I remember saying I was naughty but I didn't remember saying I was cruel.

Althea reminded me again: 'You said you were VERY cruel.' We went on to talk about whether a baby could be cruel and I didn't think that this was possible. I've been thinking a lot about what I said. It's amazing how I talked almost unconsciously while I was holding the dolls in a state of 'play', and I discovered memories and feelings that had been deeply repressed.

January 1995

I was talking about my relationship with my mother again. I don't know how we got on to it but we somehow started thinking about images — how would I draw a picture of my relationship with my mother so that it becomes clear to Althea how I see it?

I gazed out through the window — my mother couldn't be inside this special room. She is across a grassy garden sitting on a swing and moving gently forward and back. She smiles contentedly, inviting me to come and join her. I would like to join her. But the long grass that surrounds her is filled with rattlesnakes. I can't reach her. I'm not willing to try any more. As a child I was bitten on many occasions. On those days I was sad because I wanted so much to reach her; it seemed she was having such fun swinging up and down.

Today I understand that she is safe amongst the rattlesnakes — they are manifestations of the way in which she sees the world. In a way they are protecting her in the same way I used Puck to protect me.

In any case, she doesn't leave the swing, her feet don't touch the ground for more than brief moments. I'm different. My feet are firmly on the ground. Sadly, I can't have the mother I would like to have — I must give myself space to grieve for the mother who cannot be.

I also accept that from my mother's point of view she doesn't, in fact, have the daughter she wants either. (I think Althea pointed this out for me.)

While I face reality in good health my decision is to allow my mother to remain with her own thoughts as she gets older. And as I accept my mother the way she is, I can also accept myself. I no longer need to strive to be the person she wants me to be. I no longer need search for a safe path through the snakes. I am free.

Late January 1995

I told Althea that it felt as if I was moving a safety line. I wanted to move it further forward. Althea asked how we could do it. I told her that I am afraid of feathers. I admitted my phobia. It wasn't as difficult as I thought it would be.

I was quick to express a wish not to work on this. I just wanted Althea to know about it. But I asked her how she would work with it, if I had wanted to. Althea's reply made it sound so comfortable that I changed my mind immediately. We begin next week. I know there is a link between my mother and my fear of feathers.

2 February 1995

I'm feeling great. At the end of the session I actually said: 'I can't wait to see a feather because I'm going to stand on it.' What an achievement!

As we agreed last week, I just talked about some of my childhood memories. I have this vivid memory of my mother threatening to put a feather on me (I don't actually remember what the punishment was for).

I ran to the bathroom and locked myself in. After a while she said I couldn't get away and she pushed the feather through the little gap under the door. That was really terrifying for me. I put the lid on the toilet and stood on top of it where the feather couldn't reach me.

It was like reliving the experience. I re-felt the panic and the dread and the anger. Althea asked me questions like 'What are you wearing? What else is in the room?' I was recalling all the little details. She asked if there was anything, or anybody, that would make me feel less frightened while I was standing on top of the toilet. I said I wouldn't mind having Billy (my old teddy bear) with me. Althea passed me a bear very similar to Billy but I was frustrated because poor old Billy couldn't do anything to make the situation any better. I had described my shoes. Big, heavy, brown lace-up shoes that I hated, but they were, I was told, 'good for my feet'.

'So,' Althea suggested, 'if you took hold of Billy could you be really brave and step on that feather with those big heavy shoes?' Yes, yes I could! The relief was so great that I was immediately back to the present time and that's why this afternoon I'm going to the farm shop, in my boots, and I'm going to step on the first feather I see.

3 February

I am fortunate in having a caring husband. We communicate our hopes and dreams and we feel each other's pain. He is protective of me and has always sheltered me from my great fear. If a bird gets into the greenhouse he gets it out. If a feather blows into the house from an open window he removes it. We have polyester quilts and pillows and whenever we are away from home he ensures there are no feathers. We have adapted to living with a phobia and we both deny that there is a problem.

I expected David to be excited when I told him that I was working on my feather fear. But he was concerned as to whether I should perhaps leave well alone – it wasn't any great problem – and stirring it all up was bound to be painful.

So now I am confused. I usually take David's advice, he is considerably more sensible than I am. But for my own self-respect I need to do this, in what I think is probably the same way that some people have a need to climb mountains.

9 February

Discussed my confusion with Althea and established it's OK to need to do it.

I feel as if I spent the entire hour in 'Child'. I agreed to having some budgie feathers in the room; they were in a glass box. I was wearing my boots so that a feather could be taken out for me to stand on. I really wanted to show Althea my progress.

At one point when we were standing up I became aware of being quite small and for a brief moment, when Althea was holding the feathers, I saw her as my mother. Most of the time she's just there, with me.

16 March

I chose not to work on feathers today. I don't want to be just 'the one who's afraid of feathers'. I am lots of other things too.

College has been hard work recently and my confidence needs a boost. I wanted to work on roles. We agreed to use dolls.

First I had to choose different dolls for each of the roles I have in life. I chose a wifely looking doll for me, the wife, and a motherly doll for my role as mother. I chose a very shapely character for my 'Sexy Sue' role and a very sedate doll for her opposing subpersonality who I call 'Polly Prude'. There was Puck and Snow White – retrieved from an earlier session. Lastly I had difficulty choosing 'the student'. I eventually settled for someone who looked a bit like Humpty Dumpty and I'm wondering now if the student in me was feeling even more fragile than I had recognized.

Althea asked if I was going to choose a doll for the baby I once was. For a moment I rejected that idea. She showed me a new baby doll that she seemed very fond of. 'How about this one?' she asked. 'OK,' I said, and accepted it.

Then Althea asked if I would feel more comfortable if we moved any of the dolls away. Immediately I took away the baby. Althea asked why and I explained that it didn't fit and it might get in the way.

Althea suggested that perhaps by rejecting my baby part now I was doing the same as my mother had done all those years ago. Althea asked if I could take back the baby and give her a cuddle so that she felt loved and accepted. That was quite an emotional moment for me. I shall never again reject the baby I once was, in fact I shall cherish her.

23 March

Back on the feathers. I talked about the worst scenario I could imagine. It would be feathers near my face. If I was driving along and a huge bird suddenly hit the windscreen there would be feathers all around me and I wouldn't be able to breathe.

Then we talked about early memories again. I remembered going to a wedding. I was very young, maybe about two or three.

My mother picked me up so that I could see what was going on and she was wearing a feathered hat. When she lifted me up, this hat was near my face. I screamed and screamed. The more I screamed the tighter she held me and I was so afraid.

Althea pointed out that it sounded as if I was already afraid of feathers at that point. Could I remember back further, before I was afraid?

I could remember being in my parents' bed one morning. My father was dressing ready for work, I didn't know where my mother was. There was a feather sticking out of the pillow. But no, I was already afraid, nothing happened.

I've thought about this so much over the weeks. I phoned my mother yesterday and as she seemed in a reasonable mood I asked her if she could remember when I was first afraid of feathers.

She replied that I didn't have any fears or problems when I was a child. Things like that didn't start until I grew up. It wasn't until I got older that I stopped trusting her and wouldn't have feather pillows.

I just let the subject drop. If I contradict her she becomes very distraught. I imagined her swinging backward and forward. Perhaps she needed to be allowed to forget.

I can't tell anybody but I have this terrible feeling that my mother came near to suffocating me with a feather pillow when I was very young. When I was a 'very cruel baby'. When I was 'in the way'.

April 1995

I can hardly believe this experience. It's regression. I hadn't realized how powerful it can be.

I was lying on my back in my parents' bed. My mother was in the room. I caught glimpses of parts of her as she walked around the room. I could never see all of her at once, just a bit of her arm and then part of her skirt as she walked around the bed. It was a nice day because a ray of sun shone onto the bed; again, I only saw glimpses. There were no pillowcases on the pillows because they were that striped material that pillows always used to be made of. I wasn't afraid. It was a lovely day.

Althea picked up a cushion (foam filled) and asked me to bring it closer to my face. It was so real. As the cushion came closer I saw my mother's huge dark eyes and then I saw her slim fingers and shining pink nails. Then I couldn't see anything at all, and I couldn't breathe. It was real, but somewhere in the background Althea was talking to me. 'Don't stop breathing. Is it all right if I move closer and hold your arm?'

Somehow Althea holding my arm helped me to keep breathing. She asked me to tell her what was going on. It was difficult to be in two different times at once. But I was. I was experiencing the past and then coming back to the present to explain what was happening. I don't know how long it lasted.

Afterwards I was very cold, and Althea gave me a blanket and made me a hot drink. I couldn't have driven home for a while.

When I did go home my face was burning. I looked into the mirror and it was all blotched with red circles.

I kept wondering if it was all imagination. Maybe this was a false memory. When I looked in the mirror my swollen face was very real. And although it would be very convenient to dismiss this incident that I had not wanted to remember, I know it was real and I must now accept it.

April

We have spent some time discussing the regression work. Althea read me a poem that's all about how children just see bits of people and bits of furniture.

Now I'm ready to move on to the 'behaviour' bit; the bit that initially frightened me to death. I've got a sort of hierarchy of feathers. The pretty coloured budgie feathers are OK. There's a peacock feather that I actually like but the chicken feathers and the fluffy black ones are still very frightening for me. I've done some drawings of feathers and I did a little painting for Althea of snowdrops with feathers surrounding them. I think if their colours were nicer I could maybe touch them.

4 May 1995

Today I wanted to work on something different, it was a dream I had this week.

We were in the car. David was driving. I was in the passenger seat. We were somewhere, at the coast, and we came to a place where there were three forks in the road.

I wanted David to take the right fork. The one in the middle was possibly OK but I certainly didn't want him to take the left one. For some reason we were not talking to each other; all this was going on inside my head almost as if David wasn't there. We took the left fork and suddenly we were in the sea. The car started filling with water. We sat in silence. I knew at some point we had to open the window and get out of the car, but I didn't know when that time was. I wasn't panicking because I knew that David would know. This was something scientific that I wouldn't understand. It seemed we sat there silently for ages, then without looking at me or recognizing that I was there, David got out of the car. I woke up.

Althea asked me what I would like to work with and I chose a small basket of buttons. 'So,' she suggested, 'shall we try leaving David out of this dream and imagine that we just have two different sides of you sitting in the car?'

That made sense. I chose a button that looked quite powerful to be my scientific side and a more decorative button for the intuitive me.

At first I resented the powerful button, it didn't really feel like part of me. When the buttons began to communicate I recognized that button desperately wanted to be accepted as part of me. It even admired the intuitive side of me and would have taken the other road if intuition had only communicated her feelings. As the two buttons continued their conversation the power seemed to move.

Intuition is very much more powerful than I had previously known, and the scientist is more an integral part of my whole than I previously acknowledged.

I took the buttons home to keep for a while. They were a valuable experience.

May 1995

Althea has suggested that I attend a residential three-day weekend where she is a group leader. I almost declined because my wife and mother roles have always claimed weekends for themselves.

I was in a group of six, two being leaders. I felt comfortable and safe immediately, although the model of healing was completely new to me and the approach was very different from any previous experience. Throughout the first day I watched and listened to others who had been before.

At the bottom of the garden was a small lake stocked with a variety of wildfowl and, of course, feathers everywhere. The next morning I picked up a feather and carried it some way around the garden. I couldn't wait to tell Althea what I had done. Her face lit up when I told her, she was as excited as I was. We were almost there.

The next day I shared my fear of feathers with the others for the first time. It had always been very important that nobody knew. That was because nobody could be trusted. If they knew they might use it against me and completely control me. But now I was free from all those fears. Althea had asked me if she could bring some feathers into our group meeting. She lay them on the floor quite near to me.

I could feel the group willing me to abandon my fear, feel them assuring me that I was safe. One member of the group opened her Bible and began to read Psalm 91. As she read the words: *'He shall cover thee with feathers and under his wings shalt thou trust'* (verse 4), I picked up the feathers and arranged them in my lap.

It is a moment I shall never forget. There have been times since that day when I lose confidence but I can recall that moment and gain reassurance.

I went home the happiest person in all this wonderful world and in my cardigan pocket were the first feathers in my new found freedom.

Conclusion: July 1995

I have two sons whom I love dearly. Each time that I have been pregnant I hoped for a boy. I could not imagine myself loving a girl. My mother had also wanted a boy, as had her mother before her. Mother/daughter relationships have been fraught in my family for two generations.

Tace is the name I chose during my second pregnancy and is the name I would have given a baby girl. I always wondered if I could be a 'good enough' mother to a girl. I need not have doubted myself – I know now that if Tace had been born, I would have loved her.

Part Three – Comments

Through the pages of her journal you have met Tace, a woman who already had considerable personal insight when she came to me. For example, from her reading of books on therapy, notably psychosynthesis, she had identified some of her 'subpersonalities' (those different elements in her personality whose diversity was producing conflict); and a few of the 'myths' she had long believed about herself and her capabilities.

Working with someone as open as Tace, it was possible to move quickly into Gestalt two-chair work. Our first working session (that is, after the initial meeting and the history taking session) was devoted to a dialogue between herself and one of her previously identified sub-personalities. In so doing, the impish, sabotaging subpersonality became transformed into a welcome, creative one.

Over the next few weeks we strengthened our relationship and Tace got to know herself even better. One thing that Tace had known since childhood, but did not choose to tell me for two months, was that she had a morbid fear of feathers. Should she have the misfortune to be near a feather Tace would experience physical symptoms of anxiety such as sweaty palms, rapid heart beat and an overwhelming urge to escape. Tace had protected herself expertly from feathers. No one outside her family knew about her phobia as she had become so skilled at hiding it. Her family, too, had learned to step carefully round the implications of a feather phobia: even as little children her sons would remove any stray feathers which entered their home, or her orbit.

Tace's denial of the impact of her phobia on her personal and family life extended to her saying, when she first told me about it, that she did not think it worth spending time on; she had just wanted me to know about it. However, her ambivalence was apparent in that she asked how I would proceed, if we *were* to address this issue. I explained that in helping a person overcome a phobia I like to use a combination of behavioural, cognitive and creative methods. With Tace I started with some uncovering of memories from progressively younger ages, coupled with some regression work, allowing her to relive the traumatic events associated with feathers.

As a backcloth to the next few sessions I used behavioural techniques for a short part of each session. My children and I visited farms, pet shops and woods and collected a large variety of feathers. Having established with Tace a 'hierarchy' (that is, which kind seemed more frightening – chicken feathers; which least – budgie feathers and large ones with long quills, and an ordering of those in between), we spent time discussing feathers and 'reframing' them as a potentially attractive part of the world of nature, which she so loves. Then gradually and with her express permission at every stage, I introduced feathers into the room, working up the hierarchy from least to most frightening. For her part, Tace found increasingly brave things to do, starting with being in the room with them, through treading and kneeling on them to holding them. As she did so I spoke encouragingly and reminded her to stay relaxed.

Later, Tace recalled the 'archaic origins' of her fear and did regression work at a deeper level. This time other body memories were triggered, and after the session she experienced, again, the physical reactions which she had exhibited after contact with feathers for most of her life. The difference was that, this time, no feathers were anywhere near her.

As is so common when repressed memories come to the surface, Tace showed a degree of ambivalence verging on denial after this session. For me the things that gave it the stamp of authenticity were her physical, emotional and cognitive reactions during regression; and the occurrence of symptoms (body memories) afterwards. One of the cognitive factors that made the re-experiencing so vivid and real was the way in which she reported seeing 'bits' of people. This demonstrated a difference in perception consistent with infancy. Next time, when we debriefed this session more fully, I read her part of 'Animula', a poem by T. S. Eliot, which I felt encapsulated this in its description of a child's perception of its environment.[1]

Buttons, soft toys, dolls, dreamwork, regression, behavioural work, two-chair work, encouraging her artwork – these were some of the methods I used in working with Tace. She responded well to all of them, and I believe she gained a good deal from the variety.

Tace also took part in some residential group work which I facilitated, and which she found particularly helpful. Her progress with feathers had slowed. Therefore, she found the encouragement of a group of people invaluable in helping her over the final hurdle.

She had already held a feather by the time her chance to work in the group came. I collected some feathers from the grounds, so as to be prepared to continue the behavioural work which we had been engaged in on a one-to-one basis. When she indicated that it was indeed her phobia which was to be the focus, I was able, with her permission, to reveal them so that they were available for use. With assurance and support from the group, Tace achieved her goal: she held feathers nonchalantly and in multiples and even put them against her face.

After that experience Tace told me about another decision she had now taken, which had seemed impossible for her, which was to book an appointment for some dental treatment. She told me: 'Now I've conquered my fear of feathers, I needn't be afraid of anything. Going to the dentist is easy now. After all the dentist has only got a drill. Feathers could kill me!'

My initial contract with Tace involved her growth in self-knowledge. Only later did we re-negotiate our contract, in order to accommodate overcoming her phobia. I believe that there were several crucial elements in her delaying telling me about her fear: she had to learn to trust me; she had to experience the effectiveness of counselling; and she had to begin exploring her relationship with her mother. Finally, I believe it was crucial for Tace's personal development for her to get in touch with the original traumatic memory associated with feathers, and do the necessary work to overcome her fear. It was in going through all of this that she achieved her initial contract, that of discovering her true identity.

In therapy Tace made a number of important discoveries about herself, her past and her relationships. By trusting herself and me enough to face going down into the blackest, most frightening bits of her past, she made vital discoveries about the myths in her family and her own *true* characteristics.

1. T. S. Eliot, 'Animula', in *The Complete Poems and Plays of T. S. Eliot*, Faber & Faber, London, 1969.

13

INTERNAL CONNECTIONS

Case Study 2: Keith (14 Sessions)

When I first saw Keith he was on extended sick leave from his position as a vicar in a busy, growing parish. For some while he had been contemplating seeking counselling. This decision was brought to a head by a bout of depression, triggered by a viral illness.

Keith had been a clergyman for 15 years and his depression came as a shock to all who knew him. Keith's ministry was frequently described as 'successful'. Indeed, on the strength of his track record, he had been specifically asked to move to his current church in order to institute various changes, and to reverse what he saw as a spiral of falling attendance and spiritual and financial near-bankruptcy.

At the time of his institution, Keith felt himself to be facing a challenge, which, though of massive proportions, was nevertheless achievable. He set himself a number of targets to be met in the first 18 months, and reached them within a year. However, days after reporting this to a church meeting, he became ill and went on sick leave which extended for a matter of months.

I saw Keith for 14 sessions, beginning in the middle of this period. Our contract was to explore the polarities of success and failure, and to find a way out of his depression.

It was clear from the assessment session that Keith was highly intelligent, articulate and accomplished. He came across as a person who valued logical analysis and verbal processes very highly. He also regarded himself as 'different' from other people on the strength of these attributes. However, he also valued unpredictability in himself. A pet hate was that of being categorized: 'as people then think they know me and have expectations of what I will do. I dislike that and do something different, just to prove that I can't be put in a pigeonhole.'

I suspected that it would be in his best interests for him to develop his feeling function, in order to give balance to his well-developed intellect. However, it became clear at the next session that I had to pace things rather slowly at first, as he seemed on the verge of panic when I suggested he briefly use the two-chair technique in order to fully 'own' an incident from his personal history. He recoiled as though he had been hit, and exhibited extreme nervousness.

We talked about this and established an agreement that I would proceed very gently. A few weeks later, his trust, both in me and in the methods I was using, had grown to the point where we re-negotiated this contract. From then on, we agreed that I would not be *too* gentle but that, were I to overstep the bounds of his comfort to such an extent again, he would tell me so that we could keep the lines of communication open.

At the following session, Keith himself initiated work with non-verbal material. As he entered my consulting room, his gaze fell on a large painting I had recently been given by a therapist colleague who in addition is an artist. Executed in oils, this 2.5ft by 2.5ft work shows two greatly contrasting abstract scenes, divided by a diagonal line. Below this line, greyness turns gradually to blackness in an ever-darkening whirlpool. The dividing line, which is an inch or so deep, consists of patches of muted rainbow colours. Above this, an ovoid in bright rainbow colours surrounds a large, brilliant white space.

Keith commented on the picture and I invited him to look at it more closely. He drank in the brightness and vibrancy of the top half and declared that it represented Jesus' light. The oval shape was the empty tomb. He spent some moments feeling accepted into Jesus' brightness, and experiencing the relief which accompanied this.

Eventually I asked him to consider the lower half of the picture. Upon glancing into the darkness, he felt a lurching in his chest which he associated with fear and panic. He described the darkness as failure, of being 'found out': of being identified as a failure after 15 years of passing himself off as being a success. Interestingly, he also described *this* as relief, as it represented the end of pressure and demands.

This work, in which Keith *felt* the conflict between the polarities of success versus failure, proved to be a breakthrough session, providing the necessary impetus for change. Had we used only left side of brain processes, and merely talked *about* these concepts, I do not think Keith would have moved so far, and I definitely do not think he would have moved so fast. Sometimes, it is necessary to thwart a person's characteristic ways of relating, being and dealing with the world in order to provide an environment compatible with change. Keith himself talked about the need for a paradigm shift, which is exactly what a combination of creative methods achieved.

Keith arrived for his next session, his sixth, saying that he had felt very much better all week, and had noticed himself finding contact with other people energizing, rather than anxiety-provoking. This represented a huge change: Keith had spent his life regarding social contact as a necessary evil to be tolerated but never appreciated as pleasurable.

Having witnessed the strides Keith had made using one non-verbal approach, I asked him if he would like to explore his attitude to social situations using the glass nuggets. Again Keith experienced a measure of self-doubt, and said 'I'm not literate with those. I don't know the language at all.' However he decided to use the nuggets, despite his uneasiness, and set about arranging three lines of them.

Nearest himself Keith placed a single red nugget, which he said represented himself. Below this he placed four white nuggets, which he described as his achievements. Finally he placed a more widely spaced row of four black nuggets, which he said stood for other people.

Sitting back from this arrangement, which he described as 'battle lines', Keith talked about his feeling that his own achievements form a barrier between himself and other people. He said he felt compelled to talk about his achievements in any social situation, to parade them so as to prevent the horror of appearing ordinary.

Keith then began experimenting with moving the nuggets around into different positions. When he removed the row representing his achievements, he experienced the need to 'take flight', which I pointed out is one response to stress. He realized that this was because he perceived removing his achievements as letting the barrier go. He regarded this as meaning being absorbed into other people, with the result that he would lose his individuality which is so important to him. At this point he replaced the red nugget with another black one, and experienced a slightly panicky feeling at the loss of individuality involved. Finally, Keith rearranged the three rows of stones, with himself (red again) alone in the middle, with the row of black nuggets below, and the row of white ones above.

After Keith had regarded this new pattern for a few moments, I brought the large picture back into his field of vision. He saw immediately that the final arrangement of nuggets echoed the picture. This time, though, the colours stood for different elements in his life, illustrating the fluid nature of projections.

The next week, Keith was ready to work with his feelings in a deeper way. He began by describing how he feels when with other people. In doing so he used powerful phrases such as 'I feel swamped'. I decided to raise again the question of doing some chair work and this time Keith agreed.

Keith began by imagining the part that gets swamped by other people as separate from the rest of him and placed it on the beanbag. I then asked him to comfort the 'swamped' part. Immediately Keith's voice took on a tonal quality I had not heard before and he adopted a nurturing, comforting attitude. To reinforce this, he held his hands out towards the beanbag.

In order to assist Keith in conveying this message even more strongly, I said: 'Will you act that out more fully?' Keith then sank to his knees in front of the beanbag and hugged it. He accompanied this with groans, grimaces and actual straining.

When the straining and groaning diminished and finally ceased, I suggested that Keith now move to sit on the beanbag and imagine receiving an affirming hug from himself. Keith changed places but at first had great difficulty in accepting love. While he was struggling with these feelings, he imagined Jesus coming into the room.

This set up further conflict, as Keith felt so unworthy and unclean in the presence of the Lord's purity and perfection. His inner turmoil rendered him speechless and I realized that he would probably benefit most from working solely at a symbolic, non-verbal level. I proffered the basket of stones and invited him to select one which represented himself. Initially he appeared anxious, reacting as he had when I had first introduced chair work. 'It's not there!' he said urgently, indicating that no stone seemed suitable as a symbol for himself. I encouraged him to continue sifting through the stones: black, brown, white, grey, variegated, smooth, jagged, gnarled, large, small…and he finally pulled out a tiny, smooth, white one. Indicating my wooden cross, I asked if he would like to place the stone at the foot of the cross and continue communicating with God.

Another terrible, wordless struggle ensued. Veins stood out on his neck as, fingers splayed, Keith held out towards the cross his hands which were quivering with tension. Next I placed a small cushion near Keith's hands. He clearly welcomed having something tangible to squeeze and squeeze – and squeeze. He did so silently, but with immense vigour.

It is very much my usual practice to ask people to put such experiences into words afterwards. With Keith, I feared that this approach would invite him back into intellectualization, so I simply offered the white stone for him to take home. He looked taken aback. 'Seems strange' was his only comment, perhaps expressing the fact that the stone would be a bridge, spanning the two very different worlds of his everyday life and the work we were doing together.

When he returned the following week he was more animated than I had previously seen him. He described himself as 'more integrated, together, relaxed.' We both felt that another breakthrough had been achieved.

During the session, Keith again used the large oil painting as a metaphor for what he was feeling. In doing so we entered new areas, and ones which were of vital importance.

This time Keith interpreted the two contrasting images as representing his desire for excitement: to be seen as courageous and, very significantly, as a 'fighter', versus being ordinary, humdrum and showing caution blending into timidity.

As we explored these notions it became clear that the role of 'fighter' was crucial to his psychological make-up. (Incidentally, winning was not important: fighting was the key issue.) Keith described the fighter as a 'dragon slayer'.

When someone uses such an evocative phrase as this, it can be very useful to them to have the 'ground' for this 'figure' made explicit. I asked Keith about the other people inhabiting the scene he was imagining. 'Nonentities,' he said. 'Nothing else is worth considering except the dragon slayer.' Keith spent a few moments fleshing out this opinion. He related it to his attitude to pushing ahead with changes in church services. While he was explaining that he will go ahead if the majority are in favour ('Never mind an old lady who dislikes the changes'), the phrase: 'The rest are nonentities' came back to him with some force. But he said he felt himself to be in a double-bind: while he might quite wish that he could take account of the old lady's feelings, he did not dare do so as the dragon might slay *him!*

By the end of this session, Keith was beginning to voice his sneaking suspicion that in reality the 'dragon slayer' role was not so appropriate for him, after all. He had begun to wonder whether he was not really as confident as he appears.

The following week, Keith affirmed the usefulness of having been invited to identify the 'ground' to the 'figure' he was describing. He had experienced a paradigm shift during the intervening days and no longer regarded other people as 'nonentities'. This suggested to me that he might benefit from using the glass nuggets again. This time, instead of laying out bands of individual colours as 'battle lines', Keith placed nuggets in a random pattern, with himself 'absorbed, incorporated'.

As we gazed at the new arrangement together, feelings of sadness and loss welled up in Keith. He said he recalled a time when he was six years old, getting on the bus to go to school. Until then he had taken a seat downstairs, but on this day he had decided to go upstairs with the 'big boys' in an effort to gain their acceptance. (Intuitively, Keith knew that travelling on the upper deck would not be sufficient for him to be incorporated into fellowship with the others on the bus. His private school uniform marked him out as different from everyone else on the bus.) But in going upstairs he discovered that he was unable to wave goodbye to his mother, as she was obscured from view.

I asked Keith to imagine himself at the bottom of the stairs.

'How do you feel?'

'Overwhelmed.'

Keith did not know how to proceed from this point, so I suggested some options, such as setting up a dialogue with the 'big boys' or with his mother, but the option Keith chose was to imagine staying down-stairs on the bus. He did so, and felt warm, safe, confident and con-tented because he could see his mother's face.

Briefly I reminded Keith that in his present circumstances, too, he forces himself to go into scary situations, feeling different and know-ing deep down that this feeling will not be removed by the social con-tact he is enduring. In order to consolidate the healing which the new ending to the bus incident had brought about, I suggested that Keith return again to the full force of the feelings of safety and contentment, while picturing again his mother's face – and then imagine taking those feelings into his current situation. After a few moments, when his breathing had slowed and his expression had melted, telling me that he had achieved this, I suggested to him that he notice the differences from how his current situation had felt before. For about a minute he sat in silence. Again, I did not feel that it would be in his best interests to invite him to verbalize his insights, for fear of bringing this right side of brain activity to an abrupt end.

When he was back in his Adult ego-state, I suggested he look back in his imagination at himself as a child on the bus. I suggested that he see Jesus sitting next to him, giving acceptance, companionship and loving friendship. Finally, I suggested that he see himself now, as an adult, still with Jesus giving him those same things.

By this point Keith had experienced several 'breakthroughs' or 'paradigm shifts' in a very short space of time. He asked me to pray for their consolidation, and I did so, referring again to the white stone he had left at the foot of the cross; the dragon slayer and the child on the bus.

This consolidation was the focus for our next two sessions. Keith arrived for the second of these saying he was in a different state from usual, and that he was not wanting to think too much. Moreover, he found himself preferring contact with people to paperwork, which represented a massive change for him. I explained that his personality had undergone a profound shift, and his feeling of slight discomfort arose from its unfamiliarity. As, unusually for him, he was averse to *thinking*, I suggested he use the glass nuggets again. This time, in huge contrast to the original arrangement of battle lines, his achievements were no longer seen as tools or weapons – that is, as *assets* – but had now become the *problem*. His achievements had been getting in the way of teamwork: now he desired co-operation, not confrontation.

As we explored this in more detail we both came to see that, for Keith, weakness was no longer a drawback but an asset. Wondering what effect this revolution in his outlook would have on Keith's perception of the oil painting, I asked him to look at it again. Now he saw weakness in the bright, top section, which was a discovery he described as 'liberating'.

Our final sessions concentrated on consolidating the work which had taken place. Keith had experienced tremendous changes in his inner world and needed to spend time allowing his cognitive side, which was usually way out in front, to catch up with his emotional side.

A lovely postscript to Keith's story is that a few months after the end of the counselling, Keith visited the Toronto Airport Christian Fellowship, in Canada. He wrote me a beautiful letter afterwards, telling what the Lord had done for him there, and how important our work together had been, as a foundation for that experience of God's powerful healing.

Case Study 3: Brenda (Four Sessions)

Brenda is a retired civil servant who had attended a course on Christian counselling which I ran. During one class meeting she kindly volunteered to be the 'guinea pig' when I demonstrated the therapeutic use of stones. This work confirmed a nagging feeling she had had for some time that it would be a good idea to have some counselling. Generally I seek to avoid dual relationships, but am willing to offer a minimal number of sessions to students who encounter traumatic material during a course I am tutoring.

Here she describes that class session and her later individual sessions.

Part 1: Stones

My first introduction to 'stones' was during a session in a counselling course.

Several stones of various shapes and sizes were placed on the floor. We were invited to choose one, after looking at them for a short time.

In pairs, we described our chosen stone while the other wrote down what we said. I'd chosen a medium-sized flint with an irregular shape. It was black, streaked with white. This was my description:

'The stone is mostly black and quite jagged. Yet there are white streaks in it, amongst the black, more than I thought, more than I expected. However, they are not as white as I first thought.

'Some of the stone is quite smooth, worn by weathering. Yet there are rough patches and jagged edges where it's been battered about a lot and several bits have been broken off.'

At the time I had no idea that this was about projection. I thought I was just describing a stone. I was amazed at how revealing it was.

Much of my life has seemed black, but with times of lighter patches, some quite long and unexpected. These lighter times (they're not necessarily 'white') come among the blackness of depression that has plagued much of my life.

I've often felt quite battered about by life, often by forces outside my control ('weathering'?). Parts of my life have been broken off (my long marriage, my breast through cancer, my career through ill health). These have left sharp, jagged edges which are still sometimes quite painful. Yet they are being healed, being smoothed out; 'weathered' by various forces.

The class was then asked for a volunteer – someone who had a problem to solve that was not too deep.

I said I was considering whether or not to have central heating installed. Various stones were put in front of me and I was asked to pick out stones that represented various parts of the problem.

First I picked out the largest, a piece of chalk, to represent the cost – the biggest problem. Then I picked a very old flint to represent the fact that I was getting older. Next I chose a small pebble of chalk to represent myself, the only one to benefit from the heating.

Then I chose a shell with a very shiny interior. This represented all the luxury of the warmth and comfort I would feel. I thought I had finished when I suddenly picked up a piece of rough sandstone. Again I was amazed at what I said.

'This represents another part of me, a large part that feels I should be able to put up with the roughness of the cold. I shouldn't want comfort.'

I was invited to place these in any sort of order. I placed them in a circle because the problem kept going round and round in my mind. I was then invited to remove the stones, one at a time.

First I removed the large piece of chalk. 'I thought the cost was the biggest problem but it isn't. I have savings that I can use if I want to. It's my choice.'

Then I removed the flint, because common sense says that as I get older, I'll need to be warm, so why wait?

I suddenly stared at the rough sandstone. 'You're the real problem. I don't like you. You have ruled my life.'

I described how I have always had deep feelings of being unworthy, and felt I shouldn't be self-indulgent and have no right to be comfortable. 'I can see you for what you are and I don't like you, so I'll remove you.' And I did.

Later, at home, I realized yet again just how deep these feelings went. They go back to my childhood where the feelings of worthlessness and rejection were overwhelming.

I'd tried to deal with this by prayer, laying on of hands and spiritual direction. These have helped and much healing has occurred but the basic feelings come flooding back – often out of all proportion to the problem. I was angry that a simple decision like central heating should be made complex by a twisted and unhealthy way of thinking, and of feeling, that could still paralyse me.

I may have over-reacted but after a few days I ordered the central heating and made a new resolve to ask for help in counselling, to try to heal this, once and for all.

I now enjoy the luxury of central heating and the counselling has been a source of strength and healing.

It was during counselling that stones were used again. We were 'working through' my marriage and divorce. My words and feelings were inarticulate and muddled. Various stones and beads were on hand to choose from.

First I chose an ugly, knarled looking stone. It represented my guilt that my marriage had failed, that I'd let Martin down, hurt him and been selfish. I was able to lay this stone at the foot of a small cross on the windowsill, with a prayer for forgiveness.

Then I chose a pretty bead to represent all the dreams I had of marriage, some of which were realized. All the good things: the children, the kindness, the gentleness, the early years. This, too, was laid at the foot of the cross in thanksgiving.

A few days later, I wrote this in my journal: 'Today, 35 years ago, I married Martin. Thank you, Lord, for him and his gentle love. I know You've forgiven me. I hope he has. I feel so released, that knarled stone of guilt, put at the foot of the cross. And this time I *haven't* taken it back. Thank you, Lord.'

Part 2: Clay

During one counselling session I was offered some clay. I couldn't help smiling.

Five years before, on retreat, I'd been given Jeremiah 18:1–4 to meditate on. It's the passage about the potter. I was told to use my senses in the potting shed, to be there and experience it.

In my journal I wrote:

I didn't want to do this. It sounded a silly thing to do, but as I read the passage, I rather reluctantly entered the potter's shed. It looked very ordinary, with rows of different pots, all shapes and sizes but mostly large ones, all the same colour.

I could hear the sound of the wheel, squeaking, and the sound of water, refreshing. It smelt very earthy, of the ground, solid clay. I felt the clay. It was soft yet firm and I could change its shape and size with my hands and the water. I could squeeze the clay into a lump, no shape, no form, and start again, with hands and water.

Another pot began to take shape — tall, thin and narrow. I didn't like it. 'Start again!' No, not this time. Tears came. I didn't like it, didn't want to look at it. Then hands and water again and the pot was being re-shaped.

I could feel those hands, tender and caressing. More tears came as I longed for those hands and the water. Then I became angry. Angry because he wouldn't start again, wouldn't wipe the shape and the feelings away. My tears became violent sobs as I stayed with the anger. I wanted to grab the pot and smash it into a lump of clay myself. My tears became the water on the pot, marking its tall, narrow sides.

With tears rolling down my face I could hear the words, 'I will wipe away your tears.' Then the hands came back and gently, oh so very gently, re-shaped the top of the pot with my tears, opening it out, wider and wider. I shouted, 'Stop, it'll break, there's not enough clay.' The top became wider still and then it was left. My tears had stopped and I was left looking at this peculiar shaped pot, narrow at the bottom, then suddenly widened and thinned out. 'It's so useless, it can't hold anything.'

I slept. When I woke up I tried to make sense of it. The pot was me and I didn't like it. I later wrote, 'The Mis-shapen Pot'.

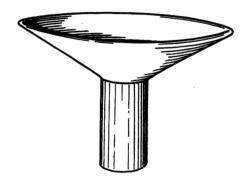

God, why did you make me like this?
What use am I, to you or anyone?
Why the long, narrow, proud base?
Why didn't you squash it flat and start again?
Or perhaps you will,
     but in your time, not mine.
And the mis-shapen pot?
It must be your shape Lord, not mine.

The next day I slipped back into the potter's shed. Those smooth hands spoke to me. 'Come on, trust me. You know it's all right.'

Fingers were drawing out clay from the inside, leaving the streaks made from the tears, outside, untouched. The clay from the inside was strengthening the thin, wide opened out rim, gradually drawing the edges together.

'But Lord, it looks like a chalice. I've nothing to give.'

'Don't worry about that. I'll supply all you will ever need.'

I curled up like a baby inside the cup and slept. I just felt peace and acceptance, not even curiosity.

Later I wrote, 'Me, a chalice'.

Me, a chalice Lord, me?

What flight of fancy is this,
That you've put into my imagination?
   Because it was you.
It was those same gentle hands.
Fingers carefully drawing clay from inside
Leaving the tear marks on the outside,
   Untouched.
You worked very carefully Lord, very gently.
There were no tears to help you this time.
But you are living water,
   You didn't need my tears.
Yet you used them to open out the pot.
That opened clay is so thin, be careful Lord.
   I see what you're doing now.
The clay from inside is strengthening it.
It's changing shape, very very slowly.
But Lord it looks like a chalice.
Am I dreaming? It's empty Lord.
'Leave that to me. Come and rest.'

My thoughts turned to the Eucharist, to the breaking of bread.

'Did you break me Lord? Break open my stone heart? You broke and gave,
you shared, giving — the chalice?

'You were broken in love on the cross. Can we only give love if broken
open? I haven't enough love. The chalice is empty.'

'Trust me. There will always be enough love.'

'Remind me Lord.'

'Every Eucharist is your reminder.'

Take, bless, break and give.
The cross, Calvary.
The chalice, stretched to its limits, broken open,
Then healed.
Stretched like your arms on the cross.
Yet my chalice, my pot, wasn't broken.
(Isaiah) I will not break a bruised reed.
Instead of breaking, you opened up,
Moulding, letting out, pulling together,
Changing;
Healing and strength from vulnerability and weakness.

So when I was offered clay during counselling, I was back in the potter's shed.

I did take some clay while I described my experience of five years ago. I found myself pinching the clay into a very thin flat piece. It's amazing how far it stretched. If it cracked or broke, I could re-work it until it had mended.

'Lord, I am still in Your hands. Your gentle, firm, moulding hands. I have been stretched – yet You were in control. Healing the cracks, reshaping the breaks. And there have been many, Lord. Help me to trust You, to mould my life in Your way, into Your shape. Lord I believe, Help Thou my unbelief.'

Part 3: Comments

Brenda's work with stones illustrates the different levels at which projective techniques can touch us. Not only did Brenda achieve (in just a few minutes of class time) what she wanted, which was to come to a decision about whether to have central heating fitted, but she also got in touch with a profound element in her psyche – a sense of unworthiness and of having no right to be comfortable but instead having to be prepared to suffer. So, as well as dealing with a surface question, this work uncovered a far deeper, more pervasive issue, and brought her to a further decision, which was to seek counselling.

This demonstrates the power of projective techniques. When Brenda carried out the initial exercise with her partner and said, of the stone in her hand, that it was 'mostly black...yet with some white streaks; with rough patches and jagged edges where it's been battered about a lot and several bits have broken off', she had no idea she was actually referring to herself. And when she volunteered to help me demonstrate a counselling technique with stones, she thought she was dealing with a surface decision but discovered a deep, early decision – 'I am unworthy'.

It was touching to see Brenda's chin virtually hit the floor when I suggested she use some clay! I could tell immediately that I had hit on something important and felt awed as she described her experiences on the retreat five years earlier. That had been done solely by guided imaginative prayer, so watching her work with actual clay gave a fitting sense of closure.

Some people present themselves for counselling at precisely the right moment in their lives. When working with a person at just that point on their journey, I am reminded of a plant in bud, turning towards the sun and opening its petals. Brenda achieved a great deal in her four sessions, largely because she was absolutely ready to make the most of it.

Case Study 4: Katie (21 Sessions, continuing)

Katie's therapy has been multi-faceted. She has been coming for counselling for about six months and together we have made use of a number of techniques: dolls, clay, dream work, stones, primal therapy and group work; they have all contributed to her journey to wholeness. Here I will describe one session in which we made use of several approaches. This could easily have had a cluttered, even contrived, feel, whereas in fact the session felt seamless, with one technique leading naturally to another.

Katie is a married woman in her thirties. At the previous session we had begun 'unpacking' a dream which I sensed carried a vitally important message for her. It took place in an office environment which Katie was visiting. Standing by someone's desk she noticed a pad with a message on the top page. Several pages underneath, a chocolate in red foil wrapping was stuck to one of the sheets. Katie removed and wrote on sheet after sheet from the pad, without disturbing either the chocolate or the message on the top page, so that the owner of the pad would not know that some pages had been taken.

At that session we ascertained that the chocolate stood for Katie's heart, and that 'the owner' was God. (Katie later realized that the person deceitfully removing 'bits' from her was herself. She was afraid of what she might have been trying to hide from God.) We had run out of time at the end, and I gave her a pad I keep in my consulting room and which seemed to fit the description she had given. I suggested that she find some way to create the image of the pad with the chocolate and which seemed to carry such import.

Katie returned the next week, saying that she had not attempted to create the image or work with it in any way. This in itself was unusual as Katie is highly committed to therapy. However, in addition to practical reasons for this such as pressure of work, she said that she was feeling frightened of finding out more about the image of the pad with the chocolate. I felt this further explained her reluctance to explore it. Sensing her hesitancy, I reminded Katie that there is no 'ought' attached to therapy: if she did not want to pursue the dream any further she did not have to. In response, Katie made a clear commitment to spending the session working with the dream, believing that she had been encouraged to do so in prayer, despite her apprehension.

Having established a clear 'contract to work' I asked whether Katie would like to create the dream image using the pad (which she had brought back with her) and some playdough. I provided sellotape and Katie set about sticking a red playdough 'heart/chocolate' to one of the middle pages of the pad. In doing so, the top part of the pad became detached from the bottom part with the 'heart/chocolate' stuck to it. This left Katie very uncomfortable as her 'heart' was now exposed. She was unsure of how to continue.

Katie then drew attention to the fact that the pad in the dream had had a message written on its top page, by the owner of the pad. Katie indicated her conflict: wanting the pad to bear a message yet knowing that, in terms of the message of the dream, it should not be she who wrote it. I hesitated briefly before offering to write. This hesitation stemmed from a therapeutic consideration: in the past, Katie had shown little awareness of the possibility of asking other people for help, and I considered using this as an opportunity to thwart this element of her process, and so wait for her to ask, rather than volunteer. However, as we had ascertained that the owner of the pad – and therefore the writer – was God, I felt that the situation was considerably more complex and decided to offer. Of course, I could have invited her to 'be the owner' and come up with the message that way, but I sensed that she would also feel very awkward about taking the role of God.

Before handing the pad back, I glanced at Katie, who was looking uncomfortable. She said she was wondering what I had written, and was thinking I might have written 'Katie is precious.' In fact, I had written: 'Katie is my special daughter and I love her very much. God.' Katie's thoughts about this seemed to indicate a discomfort, perhaps caused by feelings of unworthiness. (Katie later told me that my writing on the pad was like receiving a school report – she knew what she thought *should* be written, and what she would *like* to be written on it, but her self-esteem would not allow her to be certain – hence her discomfort. This tied in very closely with an issue which she has realized has been very significant in her development from school age right through to her current career: that of needing others' approval and love.)

Katie (imitating her dream) began pulling out pages from the pad from underneath the loving message from God. After several sheets had been removed we both noticed that the imprint of the message was no longer in evidence. I then asked what message *she* would have written, had she been writing it.

Katie set to immediately, before (with a certain amount of shame) reading the words to me. At the top she had written 'GOD.' Then there were three statements, condoning her decisions, made many years earlier, to engage in sex before marriage; marry a non-Christian; and (connected with this) to allow God to be pushed into the background. From our work together I knew that these decisions were no longer representative of Katie's beliefs and life style, and was fairly confident that she had already prayed for forgiveness for them. She then began pulling pages out from below that message. Gradually, while still removing pages, she started to express her feelings of guilt and shame. At one point, she used the phrase 'I'm cheap', which I took as a key phrase. Taking an identical pad to the one she was working with I scribbled 'Katie is cheap' and handed her the page, asking if that is the sort of message she would have expected to receive from God. She now realized that it was, and that this was why she had been so uncertain of what I might have written at the beginning of the session. I handed her a tray on which I placed a wooden cross with the loose pages and the page with the three statements from herself at its foot. She prayed aloud, then turned her attention to the playdough 'heart'. Unpeeling the sellotape as 'it doesn't need a covering any more' Katie placed that, too, at the foot of the cross.

Katie had earlier talked about knowing intellectually that she had been forgiven, yet not *feeling* the power of that. I suggested that marking the day's events in some way would be helpful. 'Then, if ever you doubt whether you have repented or been forgiven for these things you will know from the entry in your journal that on 28th March 1996 you offered this to God and were cleansed.'

Katie agreed and I recommended a burning ceremony. I brought a glass bowl and matches into the room and one by one Katie placed the pages she had torn off the pad into the bowl and burned them while praying aloud.

She took the ashes (in a plastic envelope), the 'heart' and the pad away with her as tangible remembrances of what had occurred.

In this session, then, we had continued unpacking a dream, using playdough; used an actual representation of a dream element (the pad); concretized repentance by taking symbols to the cross; and had a burning ceremony. She had not created a dream image before, nor experienced a burning ceremony, yet Katie responded very positively to the session, regarding it as another step on her journey to wholeness.

Conclusion

Keith, Brenda and Katie are very different from each other, yet creative methods of counselling proved useful for them all.

Keith's initial reaction to anything other than 'the talking cure' was of marked anxiety as, for him, the processes of the left side of the brain were very prominent while those associated with the right side of the brain carried a sense of threat.

Brenda, on the other hand, had already responded positively to imaginative work on a retreat, so was very open to the creative process.

There is a sense in which people 'learn' client skills and I knew that Katie would cope easily with the switches between symbols and methods, partly by virtue of her creative personality and partly by having experienced my counselling methods previously.

They each responded in their different ways, yet they all underwent considerable change as a result of coming for counselling. And, cliché or no cliché, God met them 'where they were'.

Counselling Keynotes

A flexible approach is vital. Be prepared to switch between methods and materials if you encounter a block of some kind: resistance or anxiety, for example.

Yet be attuned to those moments when a person's best interests would be served by being encouraged to 'stay with' a particular therapeutic tool.

Do not stick rigidly to using any particular method in any particular way. According to the principle that rules are made to be broken, it can indeed be true and therapeutically more sound to go against received wisdom than to adhere to it unthinkingly. For example, putting experiences into words is usually an essential part of counselling — but just sometimes, people who are unused to feelings may be served better by being left to encounter their emotions without being required to verbalize (which would create a shift of gear and push them back from feeling into thinking).

It is useful, too, if you can be flexible in your choice of method. For example, projective techniques to foster insight, dream work to bring resolution, behavioural techniques to encourage change — these and many others have a valuable role to play in helping people move closer to wholeness.

A flexible mind is also vital. The important themes and motifs in a person's inner journey will recur in various settings. Even while staying present with a person's moment-by-moment exploration of his or her inner world, retain a wider awareness which will allow you to notice and identify new examples of bits of their increasingly familiar 'process'.

But be aware of appearing too clever. It is generally better for people to notice connections between elements of their behaviour, attitudes, memories and feelings themselves, than to have them pointed out by the counsellor. (This applies especially if the counsellor displays a grating, triumphant, 'rabbit out of a hat' demeanour!)

It is exciting for you and the person you are working with, to find that you are building on what has gone before. A person may have been forcibly struck by a passage of scripture, or from a book; or have received a picture, word of knowledge or dream; or have encountered a particular motif or theme in a previous relationship, such as with a counsellor or spiritual or retreat director. Such previous awakenings may have occurred several years before the person comes for counselling, so a recurrence of the images or themes fosters their sense of being in the right place, doing the right thing. They (and you) may feel overawed by a God who weaves so many disparate threads into the tapestry of one person's life, and brings similar threads into the pattern at appropriate points.

14

SOME DO'S AND DON'TS OF USING CREATIVE TECHNIQUES

The essence of creativity is to create. Therefore I hope that you will take some of the ideas I have presented and use them in *your* way rather than following my suggestions to the letter.

That said, I now intend to offer some more suggestions!

1 Be Guided...

a) by the Holy Spirit

Some people who are particularly used to being guided on a moment-by-moment basis by the Holy Spirit speak of 'listening to the person with one ear and to God with the other ear'. Certainly this is a good goal to have in mind, even if there are times when just doing one or the other seems hard enough! I never cease to be amazed at the way God works. Sometimes He brings a particular image to mind which turns out to be exactly right for the person I am with. Just this week I found myself referring to the interplay of interpersonal relationships as a 'dance', which is not an image I recall using before. However it spoke powerfully to the man I was supervising, as he apparently uses the same symbol when teaching counselling skills.

At other times I feel especially drawn to suggest a specific technique, only to find out that it carries great meaning for the person concerned. An example of this is mentioned in the previous chapter. Brenda had been profoundly affected by imaginative prayer on the theme of the potter working with clay, several years earlier while on a retreat. She was extremely taken aback when I suggested (having offered few other creative materials up to that point) that she may like to use modelling clay as part of her therapy.

The precise point at which something like this ceases to be an 'intuitive lucky guess' and passes into the realms of words of wisdom and knowledge is a moot point. What *is* clear though is that a Christian's counselling can sometimes be greatly accelerated or elevated by God directly supplying information which she had not known; perhaps would not have thought to ask for; or of which even the client is unaware. A word of caution is necessary, however, Be prepared to hold on to 'words' of this kind while you offer them back to God for His confirmation, or until the person arrives at the same information by the same or other means. Be particularly wary if the 'word' relates to sexual abuse.[1] Whether or not a person in fact has experienced sexual abuse, clumsy, premature or insensitive statements by a counsellor could compound the problems and constitute 'spiritual abuse' as well as potentially creating havoc in the person's relationships.

Finally there sometimes arise situations in counselling when the counsellor may feel that he or she is trying to grab the reins of a runaway horse. Into this category I place, from my own experience, occasions when a person's need for deliverance has become blindingly obvious, times when people have begun suddenly and without warning, to re-experience their birth; and times when family tree material has intruded.[2] In each of these situations I believed that what I was required to do was simply to be open to the Holy Spirit and let God direct operations, which He has always done – magnificently.

b) by your personality

For some people who listen to others, creative methods such as those described in this book will not appeal. Earlier I referred to the Myers-Briggs Temperament typology.[3] It seems likely to me that those with a high score on Sensing or Judging may find the methods impenetrable or frustrating. S's (unlike iNtuitives) notice the fine details which their senses are exposed to and may experience difficulty in seeing (or hearing or feeling) beyond them to what they represent. The world of imagery and symbolism, in other words, is more the natural milieu of N's than of S's.

Similarly, while Judgers value order, structure and 'knowing the end from the beginning', Perceivers are happier to let circumstances unroll and evolve, and do not need to know beforehand what the final outcome will be. So the fluid nature of this kind of counselling will probably not attract many J's. Interestingly, many counsellors and leaders of churches have N and P as part of their personality 'type'.

The fact that you are reading this book probably indicates that creative methods hold some attraction for you. If, however, you have tried some of the techniques I have described, as preparation for using them with others, and have been uncomfortable or felt they got you nowhere then there may be little point in pursuing them. 'Deep calls to deep in the roar of your waterfalls' (Psalm 42:7) and you may well find yourself unable to meet another person's depths (by means such as these) if your own depths have not been plumbed by those same methods.

In that case there is much to be said for continuing with the techniques and approaches you had previously found useful. In this way you avoid de-skilling yourself and also protect those you seek to help who could be made very vulnerable if you were to usher them into places which you were unable or reluctant to enter with them. So: counsel as you can, not as you can't.

c) by the person you're helping

Matching our words, choice of symbols and the creative materials we offer to the individual we are working with can greatly enhance our rapport and therefore our effectiveness. I was counselling a woman who writes fairy tales as a hobby. She was struggling to understand and come to terms with her family background, so I suggested she tell her history as a fairy story: 'There was once a wise woman who had three daughters. The eldest was beautiful. Her hair cascaded to her waist like a wonderful golden curtain. The middle daughter was very accomplished. At balls all the young men wanted to dance with her, while her home-making skills were legendary. The youngest daughter, however, had neither good looks nor talents...'.

You can probably guess which daughter was my client! She gained considerable insights from considering her family situation in this way which, though a familiar approach, was not one she had previously applied to herself. Another person I was seeing was a young man who enjoyed woodwork. When a particularly meaningful image cropped up in a dream, he jumped at my suggestion that he create it in wood. The painstaking work he put into doing so not only helped him 'own' the image but also gave him many opportunities to (quite literally) see it from many angles, handle it and modify it. The point here is to be aware of your clients' interests, talents and skills, and be ready to encourage them to harness these in pursuit of their journey to wholeness.

Be aware, too, of your clients' major ways of perceiving and dealing with the world. If one person speaks of the way things *appear* ('I see what you mean', ' I couldn't see what she was talking about') she may well be drawn particularly to techniques relying on the visual sense. If another speaks more often of how things *feel* ('I couldn't get a handle on that', 'It was very heavy') then you may deepen rapport better by offering modelling clay or stones.[4]

2 Work Within Ethical Guidelines

Even if you are not a member of a counselling body, such as the British Association for Counselling,[5] the Association of Christian Counsellors[6] or the Association of Humanistic Psychology Practitioners,[7] I do urge you to obtain the Code of Ethics and Practice of at least one of them and determine to work within them. While it is true that codes of ethics cannot cover every eventuality they are the result of careful consideration, discussion, trial and error and of 'learning the hard way'. They constitute a framework of good practice on which we can hang our particular style. They provide safety for our clients, the general public (and ourselves!) and ensure a high degree of professionalism. Without them, boundaries easily get breached, and hurting people suffer further pain.

3 Do unto Others as You Have (Had) Done to Yourself

While professional codes of ethics do not require (yet!) that counsellors have themselves had counselling, more and more counselling courses are stipulating that students must undergo their own personal therapy, and others state that this is desirable if not essential.

In my opinion, it is having been in the 'client' chair which gives us the right to sit in the 'counsellor' chair. It is what increases our empathy, and also what deepens our self-knowledge sufficiently so that we recognize when we are reacting to a client because of something in ourselves.

In particular, I believe (as I have already said) that it is highly desirable – I would go so far as to say essential – for counsellors to have experienced creative methods for themselves before using them with others. Their use, after all, is – by definition – experiential, so when using them with others we can draw not only on past occasions of having facilitated other clients, but also on our own personal work with the materials. Then we know *by feel*, not just as head knowledge, which interventions worked and what sort of questions jarred and took us away from the experience, rather than deeper into it.

4 'I Will Give You the Treasures of Darkness' (Isaiah 45:3)

At first glance, creative methods can seem superficial, trivial, even patronizing. Just yesterday someone asked me how I work with people and recoiled at my reply, saying 'This is with *adults*? I wouldn't feel comfortable if you gave *me* toys to play with!'. Yet when people actually begin using the various materials they come to appreciate that, far from being superficial, these techniques can actually take people into deep areas.

In just a few words (for example, 'I am a…'), or after a mere few minutes of arranging stones, or making a few simple marks with a felt-tip pen on paper, the real person is exposed, stripped of his or her defences and brought face to face with a core belief concerning their personhood, situation, relationships (including with God), or their past or future.

At times it is possible to actually hear that sharp intake of breath as a person literally sees, feels or hears his or her true perception of a fundamental issue. (That is, they reach the point which my vicar, quoting someone else, once expressed as: 'I know it in my knower'!)

5 Finally, be Prepared to be Amazed and Delighted

Creative techniques can bring insight, resolution and release with amazing rapidity and in truly remarkable ways. They really can act as keys, unlocking inner doors – those barriers to wholeness. It follows, then, that as well as often bringing out people's pain they also frequently release joy and inner strength. To facilitate people using creative techniques is, I believe, to accompany them to the 'heights and depths' of their experience. As such, this work is an immense privilege for which I am deeply grateful to my clients who have shared their most vulnerable selves with me.

Postscript

In various places through both this book and this chapter I have urged caution over interpreting people's words and actions. I have just heard a lovely true story which demonstrates the importance of not jumping to conclusions. One woman I am seeing, who is in counselling training, noticed that her six-year-old son seemed reluctant to go to school one day. She knew he was due to take part in a school assembly and sensed his lack of enthusiasm at the prospect. At his next comment, her heart sank:

'I wish I was a happy person,' he said.

Keeping her own feelings in check she asked:

'Aren't you a happy person then?'

'No,' said her son, 'I'm a sad person.'

By now my client's Adult was telling her that there may be more to this than met the eye. She decided to press her son a little more:

'How do you mean, you're a sad person?'

With his reply, light dawned. Referring to the characters in his assembly he said:

'There are Sad People, Happy People and Angry People. I wanted to be a Happy Person but I have to be a Sad Person.'

Enough said!

1. Evangelical Alliance, *Allegations of Abuse, The Church's Responsibilities*, Evangelical Alliance, London, 1995.

2. Kenneth McAll, *Healing The Family Tree*, revised edition, Sheldon Press, 1984.

3. Isabel Briggs Myers, *Introduction to Type*, Consulting Psychologists Press Inc., Palo Alto, CA 94303, USA, 1987.

4. Richard Bandler and John Grinder, *Frogs into Princes, Neuro Linguistic Programming* (edited by Steve Andreas), Real People Press, Utah, 1979.

5. British Association for Counselling, 1 Regent Place, Rugby, Warwickshire CV21 2PJ.

6. Association of Christian Counsellors, 173a Wokingham Road, Reading, Berks RG6 1LT.

7. Association of Humanistic Psychology Practitioners, 14 Mornington Grove, London E3 4NS.

15

THE SPICE OF LIFE

As a child I can recall being intrigued by the beam of light from a loaded film projector. Objects on which it fell took on peculiar forms. Unexpected valleys and contrasts would appear, rendering familiar objects and people suddenly unfamiliar. It was only when that same beam of light shone onto a blank white screen that the audience could make sense of the images portrayed.

Some creative moments in counselling (or even life!) are revealed through the 'A-ha!' experience which they bring about. These will be familiar as those moments of sudden insight. One woman had been exploring her sense of inadequacy and had found a few contributory factors. Then, in one session, she used the set of small worry dolls to depict the dynamics in her family. At the end, she said to me: 'It was as though I had all the pieces of a jigsaw on a tray and only a few had been joined together. Then, with a brisk shake of the tray, all the rest fell into place.' All at once, she had literally 'seen' the hostility and distance between the members of her family and that the task she had set for herself, of holding in harmony these people and their conflicting demands, was nearly impossible to achieve. This 'failure' had produced in her a sense of personal inadequacy.

It seems to me that this is the essence of the projective techniques: to concretize that which is moving in and out of focus in our preconscious selves; to pin down the moving shapes long enough for them to be identified and so be changed.

For different people, the means of pinning down these moving shapes will vary. I have worked with a few people whose creativity is not readily expressed by any of the means I have included in this book, but instead is directed into an activity which is familiar and comfortable to them.

One woman had struggled to affirm her own identity as separate to and different from that of her parents and siblings. She enjoyed producing embroidered pictures and samplers. Leafing through her catalogue she found one picture, done in counted cross-stitch, with the words, 'Children are like snowflakes: each with their own pattern'. As this fitted her situation so well she embarked on that picture, deliberately nurturing her Inner Child each time she worked on it. The result was that she gained resolve and momentum for doing all sorts of other things she had been wanting to do but for which she had lacked motivation.

Music was the natural and familiar means of expression for another client, and his response to the emerging of a particularly profound truth in counselling was to write a song which embodied this new discovery. Another client, who has difficulty expressing his feelings in words, commented that it would be much easier if he were to use his violin to *play* an expression of his feelings. We have agreed that he will bring his violin to his next session and we will endeavour to use that to open up the lines of communication between us.

In *Growing Through Loss and Grief*, I describe some fascinating work which one man did, using unpopped corn in conjunction with glass nuggets (p. 37). Another example is that of a woman who was describing her life as a hopeless, tangled mass. She derived therapeutic benefit from discovering a lump of coloured threads among my collection of items. As she talked, her fingers teased out one end of thread after another so that, by the end of the session, the knot was already less complex. She took it away with her and returned with it the following week. This time she sat, gently caressing each of the smooth, separate threads which she had wrestled from the knotted mass. Although her life had not suddenly lost all its 'knots' it seemed that her experience of facing and meeting the self-imposed challenge of untangling the threads served as a useful metaphor to encourage and inspire her.

One of my supervisees uses swatches of material to assist clients. These can be used in much the same way as can glass nuggets, since they come in a variety of colours and do not represent anything particular.

However, pieces of material (in common with buttons) have two further advantages, stemming from their similarity to items in people's memories. Seeing a button or scrap of cloth which is very like one worn, say, by a parent can trigger fruitful reminiscences. Also, these items come in a variety of textures which can be an advantage in projective work. Clients can cast themselves as, for example, a dull brown piece of cloth, and a gregarious, high-achieving sibling as a shiny, silver one.

Your choice of creative materials to have on hand for clients to use will naturally reflect, in part, your personality and interests. For example, I am not particularly musical, and (until now!) have made no use whatever of music in the counselling room, but if music is important to you, you may well find ways to incorporate this into your work. Once certain items are assembled and ready for use, the choice of which to introduce with which client (and at what point in the work) will be mainly up to you. (Though some people make very clear which materials they wish to use: whether by a straight request or statement – 'I'd like to use the clay today'; direction of eye gaze or by passing comments – 'I've never noticed those buttons. Are they always there?'.)

In a sense, the choice of materials is endless since more or less anything could conceivably be utilized. (One colleague mentioned that, at an interview, she emptied her handbag and its contents to aid her description of why she wanted to attend the course. She was awarded a place!) The point is that creative methods rely heavily on projection, which functions, to borrow a phrase, 'at all times and in all places'.

I am reminded of teaching a group of mature students about the mechanism of projection. I asked them to choose any object in the room and make three descriptive statements about it. One man, whom I knew considered his career to be in a rut, said, 'I'm the clock. I'm going round and round in circles. I never get anywhere.' So the message is there – there is no need to purchase elaborate equipment to make use of creative methods of counselling. A pack of felt-tip pens and plain pad; stones from the beach or garden and a few odds and ends can be the beginnings of a whole new way of counselling. And I pray that the Lord will guide you as you seek to bring greater creativity and flexibility to your working practices, and that He will bless those endeavours and heal the people with whom you are working.

AFTERWORD

Since the publication of the first edition of this book, I have provided training workshops for a large number of practitioners and am grateful for the mutual learning that has taken place.

If you would like to attend a workshop or receive supervision, you can contact me by email, telephone or via my website. Similarly, if you would like therapy, or wish to make a referral, this can be arranged on an individual or group basis. One-to-one therapy can be carried out by telephone or e-mail if distance would preclude your travelling to Somerset for regular sessions. Again, please contact me so we can discuss how best your needs can be met.

Finally, should you have any comments or questions or if you would like to receive notification of workshops and other events, I should be pleased to receive them and recommend that you do so via the Contact page of the website.

Althea Pearson
Woodspring Psychological Services
Somerset, May 2007

Tel: 0871 218 1977
Website: www.woodspringpsychology.co.uk

INDEX